FATIMA:
THE
GREAT
SIGN

By the same author:

Books:

Voice of the Saints:
Burns and Oates Golden
Library Series, 1965

Heart of the Saints:
T. Shand Publications, 1975

Alexandrina: The Agony and the Glory:
Veritas Publications, Dublin, 1979

Pamphlets:

Addict for Christ:
The Story of Venerable Matt Talbot,
C.T.S., 1976

Have You Forgotten Fatima?
C.T.S., 1977

Saint of the Mass:
The Story of St. Charbel Makhlouf,
C.T.S., 1977

The Miracle of Alexandrina:
A.M.I. Publications, U.S.A., 1979

A Very Ordinary Girl:
The Story of Venerable Margaret Sinclair,
C.T.S., 1979

FATIMA:
THE GREAT SIGN

Fatima's central role in the Church, expounded by pope
cardinals, bishops and eminent theologians

by

Francis Johnston

TAN BOOKS AND PUBLISHERS, INC.
Rockford, Illinois 61105

Nihil obstat

    Fr. Vincentius Codina, C.M.F.,
    Fatima, 13 August 1979

Imprimatur

    + Alberto Cosme de Amaral,
    Bishop of Leiria-Fatima
    13 August 1979

The *Nihil obstat* and *Imprimatur* are a declaration that a book or pamphlet is considered to be free from doctrinal or moral error. It is not implied that those who have granted the *Nihil obstat* and *Imprimatur* agree with the contents, opinions or statements expressed.

Originally published in the United Kingdom by Augustine Publishing Co., Chulmleigh, Devon EX18 7HL England and published in the United States under agreement with Augustine.

Library of Congress Catalog Card Number: 80-54423

ISBN: 0-89555-163-2

Printed and bound in the United States of America

TAN BOOKS AND PUBLISHERS, INC.
P. O. Box 424
Rockford, Illinois 61105

1980

CONTENTS

DEDICATION

To my dearest wife,
Joyce

ACKNOWLEDGEMENTS

THE author wishes to express his grateful thanks to Rev. Dr. Luciano Guerra, Rector of the Sanctuary of Fatima, and Fr. Vincente Codina, C.M.F., of Fatima, for kindly checking the manuscript of this book and suggesting a number of improvements which were incorporated in the final draft, and to Reverend Mother Prioress, O.P., and the Dominican Nuns of the Perpetual Rosary, Pius XII Monastery, Fatima, for their invaluable assistance with research and constant prayers during the writing of this book. He also wishes to record his appreciation and gratitude to John Haffert, International Lay Delegate of the Blue Army of Our Lady of Fatima, for permission to quote from *Soul* magazine, the bi-monthly organ of the Blue Army in the United States, and from his books *Russia will be Converted* and *Meet the Witnesses,* in addition to transcribing important material from *A Heart for All,* including the theology of the Immaculate Heart of Mary by Cardinal (then Fr.) Ciappi, O.P., papal theologian; all three books being copyrighted by A.M.I. Press, Washington, New Jersey, U.S.A.

Thanks are also due to the editor of the *Universe* for permission to quote from an article in that newspaper on the Pilgrim Virgin statue, to Fr. Louis Kondor, S.V.D., for permission to quote extensively from his excellent bulletin *Seers of Fatima,* and for the inspirational ideas developed from this periodical. He also wishes to record his thanks to Mrs. Kay Tunstall of Tooting, London, for her generous assistance with research.

Finally a word of special gratitude is due to the Cistercian Trappist nuns of Holy Cross Abbey, Wimborne, Dorset, for their kind sustaining prayers while this book was in preparation.

Feast of Our Lady of the Rosary of Fatima,
13 May 1979

COMMENDATION BY
THE BISHOP OF LEIRIA-FATIMA

Alberto Cosme de Amaral, Bishop of Leiria-Fatima, thanks and praises all those who strive to make the message of Fatima better known and thereby lived. Among these is Mr. Francis Johnston, whose book *Fatima: The Great Sign* is destined to do much good to all who read it.

17 October 1979

Fatima has come to be a chosen place for extraordinary encounters of Faith, like so many others in the Old and New Testament. A Covenant was made, in the manner of a sacred commitment, between God and His people, through the hands of Mary, as if repeating the words of Ezekiel 36: 26-28: "I shall give you a new heart, and put a new spirit in you. I shall put my spirit in you, and make you keep My laws and sincerely respect My observances . . . You shall be My people and I will be your God." . . . Here was built a changing, praying city, made up of living stones united to the Mystical Christ, the Head of the Church, the city which has come down from Heaven, from God (Apoc. 21:2). Here has been established the Tabernacle of God among men. (Apoc. 21:3).

From the homily delivered by Cardinal Vilela of Sao Salvador de Baia, Brazil, on 13 May 1979 at Fatima, in the presence of Cardinal Seper, Prefect of the Sacred Congregation for the Doctrine of the Faith, and 208 archbishops, bishops and priests before an estimated 1,300,000 pilgrims from all over the world.

AUTHOR'S INTRODUCTION

OVER six decades have now passed since the Mother of God spoke to the twentieth century from her pulpit at Fatima. And despite the awesome nature of her intervention, which many leading churchmen believe was a fulfillment of Apocalypse 12, her endeavour to save our civilisation from spiritual and physical ruin still remains a sign of contradiction to many of those to whom her words were addressed. While millions around the world respond to her pleas for prayer and penitence to attain the spiritual regeneration of our age and world peace, others, seemingly ignorant of Fatima's extraordinary biblical and eschatological[1] significance, and contrary to the insistent exhortations of successive popes, persist in relegating the apparitions to a level where they can be safely minimised or disregarded altogether.

It is to the latter that this Introduction is especially addressed and it is my earnest hope that if they do no more, they will at least carefully weigh the words that follow against their own views on Fatima. For, before developing the main theme of this book, which is to expound the positive and indeed crucial role of Fatima today in the economy of salvation for all men, it needs to be demonstrated that the objections one hears against Fatima are entirely without foundation.

It is claimed that since Fatima is a private revelation, no one is obliged to pay serious attention to it. Others erroneously maintain that the several so-called difficulties inherent in the story undermine its validity, that devotion to the Immaculate Heart of Mary, which the Fatima message inculcates, is offensive to ecumenism, is an obstacle to union with Christ ("our sole mediator"), and has no place in this surging, post-conciliar Church. Still others regard Fatima as an essentially Portuguese affair, with only minor implications for the rest of the world. Many of these critics find the severe penances performed at Fatima repelling — though these should be viewed in the light of the extraordinary penances undertaken by the three visionary children of Fatima after seeing the vision of Hell. Finally, there is widely lacking, not a knowledge of the facts of Fatima, for these are already fairly well known, but a *realisation* of what these facts mean, of their crucial bearing on the enormous problems and perils facing the world, of the compelling need to follow through all that the remedial message of Fatima entails. It is therefore imperative that we correct these serious misconceptions and open up the profound core of Fatima (which is still relatively unknown to many in the Church), to enable us to come to close and urgent grips with the great sign given by God to our age.

It is assumed that most readers are already conversant with the basic story of Fatima.[2] Three Portuguese children, Lucia, Francisco and Jacinta, had a series of visions of an angel in 1916, and of the Blessed Virgin at monthly intervals from 13 May to 13 October 1917, in a sheep pasture near the village of Fatima, some 80 miles north of Lisbon. The children were entrusted with a message for mankind: pray and do penance for the "countless sins" of the modern world in order to save it, or Divine Justice would be compelled to punish humanity with a Second World War and the global spread of Communism in which entire nations would be "annihilated", before Russia was finally converted. The apparitions were confirmed on 13 October by the awesome miracle of the sun — as far as is known, the only time in history (excluding the Resurrection), that God had performed a public miracle at a predicted time and place to prove something. An up-to-date account of the Fatima story is given later in this book.

Before we proceed further, it is essential that we correct the dangerous error that since Fatima is a private revelation, it can be safely ignored. Shortly before his election to the papacy as Pope John Paul I, Cardinal Luciani wrote in the Italian Blue Army magazine *Il Cuore della Madre,* January 1978:

"Someone may ask: so the cardinal is interested in private revelations. Does he not know that everything is contained in the gospel, that even approved revelations are not articles of faith? I know all that perfectly well. But the following is also an article of faith contained in the gospel: 'Signs will be associated with those who believe.' (Mk. 16:17). If it is the fashion today to examine the signs of the times . . . I think I may lawfully be allowed to refer to the sign of 13 October 1917, a sign to which even unbelievers and anti-clericals bore witness. And behind the sign itself, it is important to be attentive to the elements which this sign contains . . ."

One of the Church's leading theologians, Dr. Rudolf Graber, Bishop of Regensburg, dealt with this issue in detail during his address to the Fatima Congress at Freiburg, Germany, on 23 September 1973.

"Frequently, objections are made to Fatima as being a sort of magic word in theology. Fatima, they say, is after all only a private revelation and is therefore not binding in conscience, except for the person to whom it was given. We only accept the great revelation of God which ended definitively with Christ and the Apostles. Why then such an outcry because of Fatima?

"It is to be noted that this objection comes principally from those who neither respect the great revelation of God, nor of Christ, and who even want to eliminate some fundamental truths of Faith, such as the virgin birth of Jesus, His Resurrection, His miracles, and even His very Divinity . . . It is absolutely certain that revelation as such was completed with Christ and His Apostles. What happens then if these private revelations confirm and emphasise certain truths that are found in this great revelation? This is exactly what happens with Fatima. Fatima confirms the existence of angels and of demons that Modernists try to eliminate. Fatima confirms the mystery of the Eucharist which Modernists have stripped of all meaning. Fatima confirms the existence of Hell, which is simply denied today. Fatima requires prayer and penance, values to which people today feel themselves far superior and from which they consequently dispense themselves. Nevertheless, all through the Old and New Testament, this penance is spoken of . . . Today, much is spoken about fraternity, which naturally is not understood so much on a supernatural level, but almost exclusively in the social field and in technical developments.

"Once again we affirm that revelation proper ended with Christ and His Apostles. But does that mean that God has to remain silent, that He can no longer speak to His elect? Does it mean, as some believers think, that He should remain apart and leave the world abandoned to itself? Would not this be a very strange kind of God indeed! Did He not expressly say through His prophet that He would 'pour forth of His Spirit on all flesh, that sons and daughters would prophesy, that old men would have visions in dreams. Even upon servants and handmaids, He would pour forth of His Spirit.' (Acts 2:17; John 3:1-5). Is such a prophecy to be limited only to the first Pentecost? Certainly not. Wherefore hear the word of the Prophet Amos: 'The trumpet sounds in the street, men do well to be afraid: if peril is afoot in the city, doubt not it is of the Lord's sending. Never does He act, but His servants, the prophets, are in the secret.' (Amos 3:6). Should we not thank God with our whole heart, Who even today speaks to us, especially when any danger is approaching?

"At an opportune moment, an eminent theologian called attention to the fact that we ought to distinguish exactly between private revelations which are given only to a privileged person, and others that contain a message for the Church or even for the whole world. We need not preoccupy ourselves with the first kind, but we should take serious account of the latter, since to reject them or not to be interested in them would mean a reprehensible despising of the Word of God, and a grave lack of responsibility towards the world. For these, the word of the prophet holds good: 'But what if the sentry, when he sees the invader coming, sounds no alarm to warn his neighbour? Here is some citizen overtaken by the enemy; well, his guilt deserved it. But for his death, I will hold the sentry accountable.' (Ezekiel 33:6).

" . . . Fatima represents . . . the great eschatological sign, the answer of God to the errors of the present time. The world finds itself on the eve of tremendous happenings breaking forth from the East. Hell seems to be let loose. The maternal Heart of Mary offers to save the world . . . May this depreciatory allegation, 'these are only private revelations,' not become the norm for dismissing the subject. Naturally Mary's words at Lourdes and Fatima are not on the same level as the general revelation . . . But this does not mean that God and Mary are prohibited from speaking again. God speaks once more today and in a manner all the more intelligible as His second coming draws nearer, and this is precisely what Fatima seems to indicate."

Other notable theologians echo the same theme. The Dutch priest G. Van Noort wrote in his masterly book *Dogmatic Theology* (vol. 3, p. 215):

"Such a revelation ought to be believed by both the one who receives it and by those for whom it is destined. The rest of the faithful cannot outrightly deny it without some sort of sin."

Agreeing with this truth, Fr. William A. Hinnebusch, O.P., of the Dominican House of Studies, Washington, D.C., wrote in a letter to the *North American Voice of Fatima* (10 November 1963):

"There are other things besides the solemn teaching authority of the Church that bind a person to accept something. A creature endowed with reason is obliged by his own intelligence to bow to evidence when it is present. To resist evidence is obstinately anti-intellectual. Furthermore, when reliable witnesses testify to an event or fact which seems incontrovertible, a reasonable man must give assent. To say he may refuse assent without blame is a questionable position. When a person of such outstanding authority as the late Pope Pius XII says 'the time for doubting Fatima is past; it is now time for action', then reasonable men must stop and question whether good evidence offered by reliable witnesses is behind the conviction. For a Catholic to deliberately close his mind to such a statement can hardly be without blame. If the evidence guaranteeing the apparitions of Our Lady of Fatima is examined with an open mind, the conclusion is reached that these apparitions can be accepted reasonably . . . A reasonable man accepts the evidence of reliable witnesses. When he refuses to do so, he does violence to his own reason."

In the Old Testament, God repeatedly sent the prophets to remind His people of their eternal destiny, to warn them and even punish them when they strayed from the path of salvation. Today, he sends the Queen of Prophets herself, entrusted with the same basic message: 'Pray, do penance for your sins, amend your lives, or God will be compelled to let fall the arm of His Justice.' Says Professor A. Martins, S.J. of Portugal, in his foreword to the first edition of Lucia's Memoirs:

"Fatima reminds us that wars and cataclysms are God's punishment for our sins. Does not Holy Scripture say that Sodom was destroyed because there were not ten just men in it? And Jerusalem, because it had not understood the message of peace? And what is meant by the Flood and the forty years of God's people in the desert and the captivity in Babylon? God has not changed and moreover, cannot change. Therefore what happened in the past will be so until the end of the world. Men are looking for pleasure with increasing refinements; they easily forget the lessons of history and God's commandments . . . Fatima is an alarm signal to men to amend their lives. It is also a loving invitation for sincere contrition, an indispensable way to obtain pardon of God our Father . . ."

As for several alleged difficulties contained in the Fatima story, possible answers can be put forward, as we shall see later. Those who take exception to these problems, one of which involves the mystery of the Blessed Trinity, should remember that the Bible itself contains a number of mysteries which scholars have been pondering over for nearly 2,000 years and are likely to continue doing so until the end of time. Yet no one would suggest that we reject the Word of God because certain points are incomprehensible to us. Rather we should accept what we cannot understand in Holy Writ with humility and child-like trust, remembering how Christ warned that such truths would be concealed from the wise and learned and revealed to "little children".

It is highly significant that God selected three illiterate children to convey his message to the world at Fatima. Their souls were unencumbered by the pride and prejudice that much learning can bring: they were like a white canvas on which the Divine Artist could portray His words with undimmed clarity. Similarly, an illiterate young girl who had never studied a word of theology was recently proclaimed a Doctor of the Church.[3] In the Fatima story, there are several striking examples indicating why God nominated uneducated children to proclaim His message. One of them is particularly revealing. Jacinta, the youngest of the three children, was told by Our Lady that "the sins which lead most souls to Hell are sins of the flesh." She was incapable of understanding this statement but spoke of it to her mother with the same candour and certitude that St. Bernadette had relayed the words: I am the Immaculate Conception.

The revelations of Fatima were aptly defined by Cardinal Cerejeira, Patriarch of Lisbon, as "the manifestation of the Immaculate Heart of Mary in the world of today in order to save it." From a theological viewpoint, the cult of the Immaculate Heart of Mary represents, not one more devotion to the Mother of Jesus, but the sum of all the others since it signifies the symbol of her maternal love, the expressed aspect of her person. The historical and doctrinal elements of this devotion will be covered later: our purpose for the moment is to outline the role of the Blessed Virgin in the Mystical Body of Christ, which is the Church, to enable us to appreciate more clearly the enormous significance of her intervention at Fatima. As Cardinal Marty of Paris observed on 13 August 1977 at Fatima: "There is a profound connection between Christ, the Church, the Gospel and Mary."

From the moment in Bethlehem when she gave birth to the Redeemer, Mary became the mother of all the regenerated children of Adam. Since she brought forth the Head of the Mystical Body, she also brought forth its members — all those who have been born again and those who are called to incorporation with Him. This means that in becoming the Mother of Jesus according to the flesh, she became the mother of men according to the spirit. This dignity of hers was confirmed by Christ on the cross when he said: "Woman, behold your Son. Son, behold your Mother." (John 19:27). An ancient tradition originating at the time of Origen regarded these words as a declaration that all Christians are the spiritual children of Mary.

Beginning at Pentecost, Mary has undertaken a maternal mission to her spiritual children — that of leading them to union with her Divine Son. "Her greatness lies in her being wholly Christ's and in her role of leading humanity to Christ," explained Cardinal Rossi of São Paulo, Brazil on 13 May 1969 at Fatima. It would be impossible for us to visualise Our Lady as a true mother unless she discharged this maternal role. As Vatican II stated: "Mary is a type of the Church in the order of faith, charity and perfect union with Christ." (*Lumen Gentium,* 63). The early Christians understood her salvific role well and nourished a growing devotion to her.[4] There is irrefutable historical evidence that the well known prayer, *We fly unto your protection, O holy Mother of God,* was in wide usage in the third century.[5] The cult was developed over the centuries, both in the East and in the West, like the grain of mustard seed, thus fulfilling Our Lady's prophecy: "All generations shall call me blessed." (Luke 1:48). As Fr. (now Cardinal) Luigi Ciappi, O.P., personal theologian to Pope Paul VI, expressed it at the Blue Army International Seminar at Fatima in August 1971: "The person and the mission of Mary, prefigured in the Old Testament, presented and illustrated with few but incisive lines in the pages of the New Testament, have gone on to acquire, in the conscience of the Church, ever greater splendour, thanks to the homogeneous development of the dogmas and the other Marian truths in the Ecumenical Councils, in the holy Fathers and the Doctors of the Church, in the theologians and, finally, in the solemn and ordinary magisterium of the Roman Pontiffs. With reason, therefore, can we apply to the development of Mariology the test of the book of Proverbs: 'But the path of the just, as a shining light, goeth forwards and increaseth even to perfect day.' (4:18).''

Since all Christians are brothers in Christ, it follows that the spiritual motherhood of Mary relates to Protestants as well as to Catholics and Orthodox members. "The redemption itself was conditioned upon the consent of the Virgin Mary to become the Mother of God," said Archpriest John Mowatt, former director of the Byzantine Centre, Fatima, at the above seminar. "The physical birth of our Saviour meant the moral regeneration of mankind. In Holy Scripture, St. Paul teaches that we become the spiritual brethren of Christ by Baptism. (Rom. 8:29 and Heb. 11:11-17). If this is true, then those who are baptised are *ipso facto* spiritual children of Mary. The cult of the Blessed Virgin Mary, because of her unique position as the Mother of God *(Theotókos)* has been a part of the Christian tradition since apostolic times. Both East and West honour the Virgin Mary with prayers and hymns and even with liturgical and para-liturgical offices . . . But there is no over-shadowing of Christ by His Virgin Mother, for Mother and Son are inseparable in their relationships to humanity."

When Mary gave us Jesus, she gave us all graces. This she continues to do through the mediation of her Divine Son, thus emphasising the importance and richness of His own mediation with the Father. It need hardly be repeated here that her role as mediatrix with Christ in no way conflicts with His role as our sole and natural mediator with the Father. Her mediation is clearly a secondary one which is derived from the grace of Christ. It is not an end in itself, but merely a means to an end and depends entirely on her divine motherhood by which she is a bridge between God and man. "Jesus is the only mediator of justice who can ask in His own Name and in consideration of His own merits and His own rights," said St. Bernard nearly 1,000 years ago. "Mary herself obtains what she asks through the merits of the Saviour and in virtue of prayer made in the Name of Jesus Christ. Nevertheless, such is the order freely determined by God, that Mary's mediation always intervenes in the dispensation of grace. This order admirably restores the plan vitiated and destroyed by sin, for as a man and a woman concurred in our loss, a man and a woman ought to labour together to redeem us."[6]

Crossing the centuries, we come to the declaration of Vatican II on this important doctrine. "We have but one mediator, as we know from the words of the apostle: 'For there is one God and mediator between God and man, Himself man, Christ Jesus, who gave Himself a ransom for all.' (1 Tim. 2:56). The maternal duty of Mary towards men in no way obscures or diminishes this unique mediation of Christ, but rather shows its power. For all the saving influences of the Blessed Virgin on men originate, not from some inner necessity, but from the divine pleasure. They flow from the superabundance of the merits of Christ, rest on His mediation, depend entirely on it and draw all their power from it. In no way do they impede the immediate union of the faithful with Christ. Rather they foster this union." (*Lumen Gentium*, 60).

Devotion to Mary occupied an important place in the traditions of the Catholic and Orthodox Churches and continues to flourish with undiminished vigour in the latter. Contrary to the teaching of Vatican II, there has been a certain downgrading of her cult in some areas of the Catholic Church. The Orthodox view this de-emphasis as scandalous and a serious barrier to unity. It is significant that the hierarchy of the Moscow Patriarchate in the World Council of Churches have repeatedly emphasised to their Protestant colleagues that the Blessed Virgin has an important place in discussions concerning Christian unity. Marian devotion, they stress, is not an exclusively Roman practice, but an ancient and genuine tradition having its roots in apostolic days. Russia itself has an almost unrivalled tradition of devotion to Mary, and before the 1917 revolution there was scarcely a house that did not display her icon. It is a wonderful reality that one of the most venerated of all icons in Christian Russia, that of Our Lady of Kazan, was for a time enshrined at Fatima. It now waits for the day when it can return to a converted Russia, which Our Lady promised in 1917. Originally, the Basilica of Our Lady of Kazan in Moscow stood adjacent to Red Square. In 1921 it was demolished by the communists to prove that there was no God. Since then, a number of strange mishaps have occurred, preventing another building from being erected on the site. Today the place is marked by a vacant grass plot, as if waiting for the foundations of a new basilica.

The maternal role of Our Lady has seldom been manifested so strongly as at Fatima. Later, we shall see how her intervention bears a striking resemblance to the Woman clothed with the sun in the Apocalypse. She came in 1917 to a world which had rebelled as never before against her Son and which, in consequence, is now threatened with the greatest punishment in history. But she promised to save it, by her mediation with Christ, if mankind heeded her pleas for prayer and penitence. We cannot avoid noticing here that the more her children are ailing, the more she manifests her concern for them. "Mary implores us to accept her Son's law," said Cardinal Hoeffner of Cologne on 13 October 1977 at Fatima. "She asks us to obey His law of love, mercy, purity, humility, justice and peace. The Virgin Mother is even today *the great sign in Heaven."* (Apoc. 12:1). In effect, Our Lady of Fatima echoed the Divine call to Sodom and Gomorrah (Gen. 18:32), namely, for the ten just men of this permissive age to stand up and save the city of the world.

The significance of this was underscored by the glittering star which she displayed near the hem of her dazzling white garment in all her apparitions at Fatima. This star almost certainly points to the Old Testament story of Queen Esther. The name Esther means star and she has always been regarded by the Church as pre-figuring Our Lady. In the book of Esther we read how this Jewish Queen intervened on behalf of her people when they were threatened with destruction on the thirteenth day of the month. At Fatima, Our Lady intervened not once, but six times on the thirteenth day of the month in a supreme bid to save our civilisation from ruin.

"The apparitions of Our Lady at Fatima," said the Cardinal Patriarch of Lisbon on 13 May 1972, "are an eloquent expression for our times of the role the Virgin Mary fulfills in the mystery of the Word Incarnate and of the Mystical Body. She is the messenger from Heaven who points the way to Jesus Christ, the only way, the truth and the life. She is the motherly heart who offers refuge to her children, to lead them to God by prayer and by penance. She is the cry of supplication who begs of men not to offend God anymore, for He is already too greatly offended. The Virgin of Fatima is, after all, the Virgin of Nazareth, of Bethlehem, of Cana, of Galilee, of Calvary and of Pentecost, ever eager to give Christ to the world and the world to Christ."

Tragically, there are many Catholics today who, whether by design or accident, overlook the tremendous significance of Our Lady's intervention at Fatima and convince themselves that the present dangerous world crisis can be contained and perhaps resolved by physical action such as *détente,* disarmament, pacifism, economic aid and so on. They fail to recognise that the crisis is essentially a spiritual one which can only be solved by the sword of the spirit. For instance, while it may be salutary to deplore the crushing burden of the arms race, the answer is not to campaign for unilateral disarmament, which would expose us to even greater peril, but to strive to remove the cause of the arms race, which is sin.

Speaking at the above seminar, the celebrated philosopher Abbé André Richard, D.D., editor of France's prestigious newspaper *L'Homme Nouveau,* said: "It is important to affirm that reconciliation between Christianity and Soviet Russia, from points of contact and meeting ground that we have accepted, is made impossible by communist rulers. This has its roots in the heart, not in reason. And it is to be found in our Western countries as a communist export. It can only be explained by that power which Jesus indicated as the Liar, homicidal from the beginning. It does not want God to exist because it does not wish to depend on any power outside itself.

"We can overturn this satanic position only in the spirit and the participated grace of the Immaculate Heart of Mary expressed in these words: "Behold the handmaid of the Lord, be it done unto me according to your word." (Luke 1:38). The Virgin came to Fatima to offer us the power of a humble heart full of love and of obedience with which Jesus endowed the Heart of his Mother. The reparative Communion of the First Saturdays of the month and the consecration of the world, so expressly implored by her, have that profound significance. Jesus wishes that the Heart of His Mother and His be honoured. And we priests of the Church sometimes do so little to bring this about! We try to fight Satan without the necessary spiritual arms . . . For it is to every bishop, to every priest, and to every member of the faithful, that the Mother of Jesus addressed herself. She asked us for a renewed and personal intimate union to her Heart, that Heart which the Holy Spirit has joined indissolubly to the Heart of Jesus in order that the life of the Father could be communicated to every creature according to the perfect mode of the unity of the family of God.

"Thus, in the presence of a supernatural call consonant with traditional Christianity and the exhortations of the authorities of the Church, every one of us must ask himself: On the spiritual battle-front (that of prayer, of intimate offering in union with the two hearts, of true conversion), what do I bring to my beloved Russian brothers? In what can they count on me in order that the grip of Satan (which our sins have given a free hand) can at last be loosened from them? What am I doing in order that Soviet rulers might acknowledge the right of every Russian to religious information, in order that all our brothers of Russia, penetrated by a knowledge of the gospel, may realise their great apostolic potential energy for the reign of God?"

The apparitions of Fatima have long received the official approbation of the Church. On 13 October 1930, the Bishop of Fatima, Dom José Correia da Silva, published his Pastoral Letter on the cult of Our Lady of the Rosary of Fatima which completed seven years of painstaking enquiry by an official canonical commission of investigation. After briefly summarising the events of 1917 and the reasons for his decision, he ended:

"We judge it well:

1. To declare worthy of credence the visions with which the children were favoured at the Cova da Iria, in the parish of Fatima, diocese of Leiria, on the 13th of each month from May to October 1917.

2. To authorise officially the cult of Our Lady of Fatima."

The following year, 300,000 people made a national pilgrimage of thanksgiving to the growing shrine and the entire Portuguese hierarchy solemnly consecrated their country to the Immaculate Heart of Mary. On 13 May 1938 they renewed the consecration in the presence of 20 prelates, over 100 priests and half a million pilgrims in thanksgiving for Portugal's preservation from the Spanish Civil War. Pope Pius XI manifested his belief in the apparitions on a number of occasions, but it was left to his successor, Pope Pius XII, to take the first formal step towards compliance with Our Lady of Fatima's request for the consecration of Russia by the Pope in union with all the world's bishops. Known as the 'Collegial Consecration', this unprecedented act was promised to be the means by which Russia would be converted. Since this important subject has engendered much controversy and misunderstanding, we shall be clarifying it at length later in this book.

On 31 October 1942, Pope Pius XII consecrated the world to the Immaculate Heart of Mary. Two years later the Pontiff, who admitted that "Fatima is the summation of my thinking" and who was called "the Pope of Fatima", instituted the Feast of the Immaculate Heart of Mary and on 13 May 1946, solemnly crowned a statue of Our Lady of Fatima and proclaimed her Queen of the World. During the closing ceremonies of the 1950 extended Holy Year at Fatima, Cardinal Tedeschini, the papal legate, told the immense crowd gathered at the shrine that the Pope had seen a repetition of the 1917 solar miracle in the Vatican on the eve and octave of the promulgation of the dogma of the Assumption.

"Was this a reward?" His Eminence asked. "Was this a sign of sovereign Divine pleasure for the definition of the Assumption? Was this a heavenly testimony authenticating the connection between the wonders of Fatima and the centre, the head of Catholic truth and teaching authority? It was all three together."

A few days later, the Vatican newspaper *L'Osservatore Romano* of 17 November 1951 commented:

"It is not our task to formulate deductions from these singularly analagous events (the original solar miracle and its repetition for the Holy Father), but the intervention of the Most Blessed Virgin is frequent in the gravest days of the history of the Church, even with intimations to the successor of Peter personally".

The following year on 7 July 1952, Pope Pius XII consecrated Russia to the Immaculate Heart of Mary, though without the participation of the bishops. His successor, Pope John XXIII, instituted the Feast of Our Lady of the Rosary of Fatima and termed the apparitions "the centre of all Christian hopes." On 21 November 1964, Pope Paul VI solemnly renewed the consecration of the world to the Immaculate Heart of Mary in the presence of all the bishops assembled at the Second Vatican Council, and announced a mission to convey the Golden Rose to Fatima. Three years later, on the occasion of the golden jubilee of the apparitions, His Holiness journeyed to Fatima "as a humble pilgrim" to "pray for peace" in the presence of a million pilgrims from all over the world.

Today, Fatima stands as a shining symbol of hope in a world dominated by the spectre of mass apostasy from God and its awful shadow of the nuclear bomb. "Our only hope for world peace is found in the message of Fatima", declared Douglas Hyde, the ex-communist journalist.[7] Echoing his words, Archbishop Fulton Sheen wrote shortly afterwards: "Devotion to Our Lady of Fatima is actually a petition to save man from nature made destructive through the rebellious intellect of man."[8] And again: "How shall we overcome the spirit of Satan except by the power of that Woman to whom Almighty God has given the mandate to crush the head of the serpent?"[9]

This, then, is the setting for the awesome drama that constitutes the theme of this book.

NOTES

1. Eschatological — dealing with the four last things: death, judgement, Hell and Heaven.
2. The most authoritative account of the Fatima story is Lucia's Memoirs, published as *Fatima in Lucia's own words* by the Postulation Centre, Fatima, Portugal, in 1977, and available in the U.K. from Augustine Publishing Co.
3. St. Catherine of Siena.
4. cf., *An Essay on the Development of Christian Doctrine* by John Henry Newman, Section 2, Chap. 4, which cites many examples.
5. cf., 5th Mariological Congress, University of Lisbon, 2 August 1967, under the Presidency of the Cardinal Patriarch of Lisbon.
6. This teaching is particularly stressed by St. Bernard in *Sermo in Dom. Infra Octav. Assumptionis,* No. 2. The doctrine was confirmed in January 1921 by an Office and Mass in honour of Mary Mediatrix, which Pope Benedict XV granted to the dioceses of Belgium and to all the dioceses of the world that should request it.
7. Address in Lisbon, 10 October 1951.
8. *Life is Worth Living,* Second Series, "Fatima", p. 87n.
9. *The World's First Love,* Chap. 22.

I

ALTAR OF THE WORLD

THE shrine of Fatima lies high up in the rugged, pine-clad ranges of the Serra d'Aire mountains of central Portugal. Despite its remote location (Lisbon is 90 miles to the south and the nearest railway station is 16 miles distant), scores of cardinals, archbishops and bishops, thousands of priests and millions of ordinary people from all over the world flock there each year to pray at the hallowed spot where the Mother of God appeared in an "explosion of the supernatural", to borrow Claudel's vivid phrase, and spoke words of warning and hope to our tumultuous century.

Over the past thirty years or so, the shrine has mushroomed around the towering white Basilica of the Rosary and the adjacent Cova da Iria, a vast natural amphitheatre in which the visions took place, so that it now dwarfs the small dusty town that bears its name. The latter has little of the modern trappings and gaudy commercialism seen elsewhere. Hotels and hostels are growing, but the majority of pilgrims, being Portuguese and thoroughly imbued with the penitential spirit which characterises Fatima, sleep under the stars in the Cova da Iria, or camp out here and there in the undulating, rock-strewn fields amid straggling olive groves and fig trees. The prevailing atmosphere of austerity infects young and old alike of all social classes and is heightened by the extremes of temperature experienced at an altitude of 1,200 feet — fiery hot summers and torrential autumn rains which the bronzed, weather-beaten Portuguese pilgrims seem to bear with a stoical nonchalance.

Some sixty religious Orders and Congregations have established themselves at the shrine, in addition to numerous seminaries, houses for retreat and days of recollection, and fully-equipped centres for the great international congresses, seminars, ecumenical meetings and pastoral conferences regularly held there. Recent years have witnessed two particularly significant gatherings: *Fatima in the light of Vatican II,* a major international seminar held in 1969 in which many eminent prelates participated under the presidency of Cardinal Ursi of Naples, and *The Immaculate Heart of Mary in the Apparitions of Fatima,* another great international seminar held in 1971 and attended by the Car-

dinal Patriarch of Lisbon and a number of leading theologians and
lay activists. The principal speaker, Fr. (now Cardinal) Luigi
Ciappi, O.P., personal theologian to Pope Paul VI, expounded the
theology of the Immaculate Heart of Mary which is substantially
recorded later in this book.

Fatima is also a highly-esteemed seat of learning. Among the
important educational institutions there are the Centre of Studies
catering for some 300 students annually, and the well known
Institute of St. Thomas Aquinas staffed by the Dominicans, whose
summer course in theology attracts hundreds of priests, religious
and students yearly. Study Weeks of a religious, cultural, educational and professional nature are held regularly in the Sanctuary.

The immense pilgrimages which take place at Fatima on the
13th of the month from May to October are, perhaps, unprecedented in church history. Crowds numbering up to half a
million people, many having walked hundreds of miles, gather in
the Cova da Iria to commemorate the apparitions, manifesting a
faith, devotion and humility that is almost extinct in the world
today. On the night of 13 October 1960, 500,000 prayed right
through till the morning in union with all-night vigils of reparation
held in some 300 dioceses around the world. Seven years later, an
even greater multitude, including Pope Paul VI, gathered in the
Cova da Iria to commemorate the golden jubilee of the apparitions — an indescribable spectacle of fervour and faith. In 1969,
the millions of pilgrims arriving in Fatima came from 53 countries
and included 4 cardinals, and scores of archbishops and bishops,
resulting in 32 large concelebrations and over 10,000 Masses in the
Cova da Iria.

The numbers continued to grow despite inflation and financial
crises in many countries: in 1975, when the communists seemed on
the verge of seizing power in Portugal and the shrine was
threatened with bomb attacks to deter pilgrims, record crowds
poured into Fatima like a tidal wave and united in an overwhelming cry of supplication to Our Lady. Typical among the
countless throngs of pilgrims were forty-nine different groups from
the distant Philippine Islands. One of the last of these was led by
Cardinal Rosales of Cebu, who left the following message
inscribed at Fatima:

"We have come to this sanctuary of the Virgin of Fatima, full of
confidence that she will bless us and grant us the grace we ask:
peace for the world and that her Immaculate Heart will triumph in
these calamitous times. We are deeply impressed by the devotion
of the people who come to pray in this sanctuary. We promise to
pray the rosary every day as Our Lady desires."

Significant among the vast groups regularly converging on
Fatima are the Armed Forces pilgrimage, the annual Pilgrimage of

Penance from the distant town of Guarda in which thousands participate, walking the last miles of the way and fasting on bread and water, and the inspiring Children's Pilgrimage which attracts up to 250,000 youngsters with their teachers and families each year. The organisers of the latter event receive the full co-operation of the government, TV and radio. Pamphlets on living the Fatima message are circulated in advance to all schools in Portugal and the resulting, highly organised pilgrimage is one of the most moving spectacles seen at the shrine. "It was to children that Our Lady spoke", that was the theme for all pilgrimages to Fatima during the 1979 International Year of the Child.

Orthodox and Protestant pilgrimages are also attracted to Fatima. In 1970, a number of Orthodox prelates led by Metropolitan Emilianos Calabre, official representative of Patriarch Athenagoras, arrived in the Cova da Iria to pray for Christian unity. That same year also saw His Holiness Vasken I, supreme head of all Armenians separated from Rome, praying for unity at the shrine after meeting with Pope Paul VI. Non-Christians too feel drawn to this haven of peace, for its message of hope stirs the deepest yearnings of the human spirit. In 1969, a Buddhist pilgrimage came all the way from Japan to pray at the shrine, hearing Mass at the Chapel of the Apparitions with a recollection that was edifying.

The pilgrim throngs arriving in Fatima on weekends now frequently exceed the numbers who came on the thirteenth of the month twenty years ago. In April 1976 for instance, the multitudes included the entire Portuguese Episcopate, 700 religious of the Franciscan Hospital Sisters, over 200 superiors of religious communities, 1,000 members of the Hope and Life movement for widows, 100 priests of the fast-growing Marian Movement of Priests, and 3,500 catechists led by Cardinal Ribeiro of Lisbon, who came to prepare for a synod on catechesis.

"The Cova da Iria is truly the altar of the world," the Cardinal said on 13 May 1972. "Coming from all over the earth and distinguished by varying types of culture, we are gathered together to offer thanksgiving and supplication on this holy mountain . . . Today as yesterday, Fatima fulfills a relevant role in the history of the contemporary Church, in Portugal and in the world. The apparitions of Our Lady here contain inexhaustible spiritual riches. The messenger who came down to the Cova da Iria is the Mother of God who, according to Vatican II (*Lumen Gentium,* 54), occupies a place in the Church which is the highest after Christ, and yet very close to us."

On 13 May 1974, His Eminence underscored to the vast crowd in the Cova da Iria the meaning of their pilgrimage and the lofty ideal that Fatima signifies.

"We come here, the better and more clearly to hear and meditate on the voices that reach us from Heaven and from earth. Those of earth . . . speak of renewal, of human life shared in liberty and responsibility, of union of efforts in the building of a new world where reigns truth and justice, love and peace. The voices from Heaven come down to meet these, to impress on us the constant necessity of changing our lives, of converting our hearts, of the reform of social structures and fraternal reconciliation between men, who are all children of the same God. Everyone needs renewal. We all need to be converted from sin to grace. We are all sinners, and if we truly place ourselves before Christ, none of us would have the right to cast the first stone . . . The Holy Virgin of Fatima asks us to amend our lives and not to offend the Lord anymore, for He is already too greatly offended."

His Eminence added: "From the very beginning, Fatima was always the hope of peace. Untold thousands have come here to implore this precious gift from God. We look to the maternal protection of Our Lady of the Rosary of Fatima . . . Together with Pope Paul VI we may well say: 'The Catholic Church, endowed with centuries of experience, recognises in devotion to the Blessed Virgin a powerful aid for man as he strives for fulfillment. Mary, the New Woman, stands at the side of Christ, the New Man, within whose mystery the mystery of man alone finds true light'."

Shortly before the 13th of the great months of May to October, columns of sunburnt pilgrims can be seen steadily plodding along the unshaded shoulders of endlessly winding roads, scores and even hundreds of miles from Fatima, weighed down with baggage, their faces set and serene, now and then breaking into a hymn, the inevitable rosary in their hands swinging to the measured tramp of their feet. They seem instinctively aware that life itself is a pilgrimage and that each day brings them a step closer to their eternal destiny. From all points of the country they converge on Fatima, "walking day after day, praying and singing, coming from all the different cities, towns and villages," as Cardinal Sales of Rio de Janeiro graphically described them on 13 May 1973. "They belonged to every social class, sleeping on the bare ground, patiently facing the sun and rain, to respond to Our Lady's appeal: 'Do penance.' I witnessed it all. Even the throngs that flocked in by bus and car showed nothing but reverence in their demeanour. There was a sense of the spiritual all around. No one could deny the religious aspect in evidence in its deepest concept — united to the cross of Christ, praising the Son and acclaiming the Mother. I saw the real Fatima. I felt deeply united to the Pope and to the hierarchy, to the Spirit of God that breathes where He wills. I felt the strength of a pastoral activity that seeks to correct flaws, but does not destroy; that prunes, but does not cut down the tree; that is faithful to the essential and leaves aside what is accessory. Fatima has a great mission to the world today: the reconciliation of men, to be brought to God by Mary, the Mother of God and our Mother."

By the afternoon of the 12th most of the pilgrims have reached their goal, the promised land of the Cova da Iria, flowing with the milk and honey of divine grace. Their numbers are swollen by hundreds of packed coaches arriving from the cities of Portugal and from Spain, France, Germany, Italy and elsewhere. They mingle with thousands of pilgrims who have flown in from the British Isles, North and South America, Asia and Australia, and the hardy stalwarts who have made the arduous 18-hour train journey all the way from Irun on the Spanish-French border. Most of the foreign pilgrims find accommodation in the many religious and boarding houses in addition to the few hotels. The air is filled with the subdued chatter of many languages, the cries of excited children, the incessant crunching of heavily-laden cars, caravans and coaches being adroitly manoeuvred and parked bumper to bumper, the ubiquitous smell of camp-stove cooking which pervades the surrounding fields like an alien incense.

By evening the Cova da Iria is a fast-filling reservoir of humanity. Thousands pour in from all sides like an incoming tide, disciplined, silent and recollected, many covering the last quarter of a mile on their knees. In successive waves they converge on the Chapel of the Apparitions which enshrines the spot where the Blessed Virgin appeared in 1917, manifesting an extraordinary attitude of devotion. Hundreds of others move across the square or round the little Chapel on bandaged knees, as if summoning the last ounce of sacrifice from their weary bodies. Here and there one sees tough soldiers in battledress, long-haired teenagers in jeans, smartly-dressed European and American pilgrims, negroes and orientals, swarthy old peasant men with their aged wives draped in black shawls, colourfully dressed children gathered round their bowed parents — all of them kneeling or standing under the fiery sun or in torrential rain, praying unceasingly. No priest has ever asked anyone to undertake such exceptional penances. These heroic souls are impelled by a vibrant love of God which seems to know no limits. They appear to have penetrated to the heart of the Fatima message and understood to the full those trenchant words of Jacinta that deserve to be shouted from the housetops of this pleasure-seeking world: *"If men only knew what awaits them in eternity, they would do everything in their power to change their lives."*

And Cardinal Sales commented: "I thought of the foolishness of those who oppose these manifestations or minimise them. I thought what a crime they commit. Tears ran down the cheeks of many of the pilgrims, silent tears that portrayed a spirit of penance in union with Christ. They came because of His Mother. Union with the redeeming cross can be seen as one of the characteristics of their devotion." Echoing his words, Cardinal Baggio, Prefect of the Congregation of Bishops, had this to say on 13 May 1976 in the Cova da Iria: "Our Lady seems to repeat unceasingly to these self-less pilgrims, as to us likewise who feel ashamed in the face of such generosity and such sacrifice, the solemn proclamation of her Divine Son: 'The Spirit of the Lord has sent me to bring the good news to the poor, to heal the contrite of heart.'" (Luke 4:18).

The intense silence around the little Chapel is punctuated by the strains of the Fatima *Ave* which is sung with a rousing fervour. As night falls, the torchlight procession begins around the statue of Our Lady of Fatima and the immense esplanade becomes a sea of flickering lights of overpowering splendour. Concelebrated High Mass follows in the open, at the end of which the vast crowd gathers around the Blessed Sacrament exposed in front of the Basilica for an all-night vigil of reparation, or settles down on the hard ground or under the spacious colonnades of the great Basilica for a few hours of fitful rest.

Writing in the Vatican weekly *Osservatore della Domenica* in the 1960s, the famous Jesuit preacher Fr. Lombardi described his experience one night in the Cova da Iria. "People who have travelled long distances and barefooted rest under the colon-nades. They fulfil their promises with a fidelity that would make the sceptic tremble . . . I spoke at the night vigil and was seized by a thought that came to me like a revelation, that moved me even to tears. Believe me, I wept. Now I am not one easily moved to tears. The thought was this: in Fatima, Our Lady had asked something of mankind. I felt that today, men could respond to her with a deter-mined will to be oriented through all the ways possible for a better world."

And Cardinal Sales commented on 13 May 1973: "The effect of this truly authentic miracle, the apparitions of Fatima, could be strongly felt. Here were the people of Portugal and of other countries transmitting a message of faith to the world today. Hundreds of thousands thronged the Cova da Iria, calm and recollected, spending the night in the open, breathing an atmosphere of prayer and penance. It was an unforgettable lesson by the people of God. This is something extraordinary for a world that is held to be estranged from God. All the force of the super-natural in its right and adequate concept, is truly present here." And his Eminence added with moving eloquence to the 700,000 pilgrims listening to him, including 3 other cardinals, 15 bishops and over 100 priests: "Fatima is a repetition of the tenderness of Christ shown on the cross. (John 19:20). From there He gave Mary to us and here He gives salvation at a difficult moment for His Church. This is a holy and venerable place for the whole people of God. Fatima has become a sign raised up in the midst of this unbelieving generation. It is a sign of conversion, of penitence, of paschal faith, of new hope for humanity redeemed from sin."

It must never be forgotten that the prayers and arduous penances offered up in the Cova da Iria benefit each one of us through the Communion of Saints, as we shall discuss fully later. They also benefit mankind in general and particularly the cause of world peace. This fact is of crucial importance today when efforts are being made by certain elements in the Church towards the attainment of peace by essentially physical means, while relegating prayer and penitence and excluding all reference to the Queen of Peace. Their efforts imply a tacit rejection of the scriptural basis of peace, and are doomed to futility in advance, for no human contrivance or ingenuity is capable of securing peace, which is a gift from God through the intercession of Our Lady. When at the height of the First World War Pope Benedict XV urged the Catholic world to implore Our Lady to intercede with her Divine Son for the gift of peace, the Blessed Virgin responded just eight days later by appearing at Fatima and giving us her Peace Plan from Heaven. And God certified her words with His own fiery signature in the sky. Surely these advocates of peace are not presuming to know better?

Pope John XXIII termed the Fatima message "the world's greatest hope for peace." And speaking to a million pilgrims in the Cova da Iria on 13 May 1967, Pope Paul VI said: "We have come to the feet of the Queen of Peace to ask her for the gift of peace which only God can give." Underlining these words, Cardinal Carberry of St. Louis told hundreds of thousands of pilgrims at Fatima three years later: "If there is one word that would distil the essence of the Fatima message, it is peace. If there is one cry that arises from a restless and tormented world today, it is the cry for peace. Is this universal desire for peace based on an illusion? To be honest with ourselves, we must admit that the goal of peace, humanly speaking, seems almost unobtainable. Our generation, and indeed the generation before us, has scarcely known a year without the agony of war in some part of the world. If peace is to be won, it must be won with the sword of the spirit . . . In the name of all of us here, I turn to Our Lady and I pray, as Pope Paul before me has prayed: Mary, Queen of Peace, obtain for us peace of soul, obtain for us peace in our nations, obtain for us peace in the world."

On the morning of the 13th, the crowds gathered in the Cova da Iria reach their maximum size and solemn High Mass is concelebrated on a special outdoor platform erected in front of the

Basilica. There follows the blessing of the sick and the imploring invocations of countless thousands, echoing the cries that rose from Palestine 2,000 years ago: Lord, he whom You love is sick! Lord, if You will, You can make him whole! Lord that I may see! Lord that I may hear! Lord that I may walk! Sometimes there is a dramatic cure. American Blue Army leader John Haffert described how he witnessed two spectacular miracles in the 1940s, one of which involved a woman on the point of death from a malignant brain tumour.[1] On 13 August 1968, the finger of God flashed down twice in a few moments; two paralytics rose from their litters and walked to the stupefaction of the crowd.[2] Another notable cure a few years earlier involved the instantaneous recovery from paralysis of a young boy in the Chapel of the Apparitions. The child got up and walked before his parents' eyes, moving hundreds of speechless onlookers to tears.[3]

The most common cures, of course, are spiritual ones — the return of countless prodigal sons to their Father's house. As Cardinal Ferdinand Cento said at Fatima on 13 May 1965: "We come to Fatima to be purified. We come to be changed from listless, lukewarm Catholics into fervent apostles. From Fatima, we should depart by another way, renewed and transformed."

Fourteen years later, Pope John Paul II endorsed the same theme in a message to the Bishop of Fatima on 13 May 1979: "Conversion is at the centre of the message of Fatima. It is a continual commitment to seek and bear witness to 'deep knowledge of God and of Jesus Christ our Lord,' the way of eternal life (cf. John 13:3), which necessarily passes through penitence (cf. Luke 13:3) and through prayer (cf. John 15:5), which is for the Church in our days more than a need. It is a categorical imperative. For this reason, a pilgrim with the pilgrims to Fatima, I exhort you to pray to Mary, through Mary and with Mary, Holy Mother of God and Mother of the Church and Our Lady Help of Christians, trusting in her fullness of grace, manifesting to her filial love and sincere devotion based on a resolution of faithfulness to Christ, faithfulness to the Church and faithfulness to men our brothers."

Yet despite the ever-widening response to Our Lady's message of prayer, penitence and amendment of life, despite the official approval of the Church in 1930, Pope Paul's pilgrimage to the shrine in 1967, the relentless fulfillment of the prophecies made by Our Lady there, the wave of holiness generated by the great apostolic movements of Fatima: despite all these impressive factors, the prodigy of Fatima is continually assailed by alien voices and certain foreign publications riddled with falsehoods. But one has only to glance at the vast sea of praying humanity in the Cova da Iria, to learn of the miracles of grace and conversion witnessed there by so many priests, and in particular, to read of the thousands of Fatima devotees making monthly all-night vigils of reparation around the world, to realise where these attacks originate. "I will place enmities between you and the woman, between her offspring and your offspring." (Gen. 3:15).

Nor is there any substance in the view occasionally expressed that Fatima is characterised by the misguided piety, sentimentality and emotional excess which occasionally motivate mass movements. The fervour of the pilgrims is manifestly deep and genuine as they pray for hours on end and perform severe penances with a humility and love of God that would make their armchair critics wither. "They come to pray to our heavenly Father through Jesus Christ in union with Our Lady who is interceding with us," as Cardinal Koenig of Vienna said at Fatima on 13 May 1975. They have heard with the more sensitive understanding of children the voice of the Mother of the Church, echoing those fundamental words of her Divine Son: *Pray always . . . Unless you do penance, you will all likewise perish.* As Bishop Humberto Mozzoni, Apostolic Nuncio in Buenos Aires, wrote in the Book of Honour at Fatima in 1968: "To come to Fatima, to the feet of the Virgin, is to live the serenity of Heaven. It is to feel the vital living of the spiritual values of the Church."

This growing response to the message of Our Lady of Fatima, not only at the shrine, but throughout the world, is a key factor in resolving the present crises in the Church and the world. And as the response increases, we can expect the enemy to intensify his opposition as he sees his time growing short, until both crises become acute. It would be idle to speculate on what lies in the immediate future: the many prophecies of saints and seers which seem to relate to our times must, perforce, be taken with reserve. The only certainty is that an unprecedented triumph of the Mother of God is fast approaching which will usher in the conversion of Russia and world peace. This will mark the beginning of the Age of Mary foretold by St. Louis de Montfort, according to Sister Lucia, the last survivor of the three children to whom Our Lady appeared at Fatima.

Before summarising all this however, we need to review briefly the story of the Fatima apparitions in the light of our present knowledge. Certain aspects of the events of 1917-29 which hitherto remained blurred or obscure, have been brought into sharp focus by the advancing lens of time. Contributing to this clarifying trend have been the disclosures by Sister Lucia in 1967 and 1973, the resolution by competent theologians of several supposed difficulties, and the clearer perspective of history. We shall also need to discuss in some detail the five essential elements of Fatima, viz., the vision of Hell, the prophecies of Our Lady, the solar miracle, the Collegial Consecration of Russia to the Immaculate Heart of

Mary (which is to be the means of the conversion of that country), and finally, the all-important message which the Blessed Virgin delivered to the world, which Pope Pius XII acknowledged as "the summation of my thinking."

NOTES

1. cf. *Russia will be Converted,* by John Haffert, A.M.I. Press, Washington, N.J., U.S.A., 1958.
2. This double miracle occurred in the Basilica during Mass. cf. *Seers of Fatima,* 4/1968.
3. Recorded in *Seers of Fatima,* 5/1966.

II

ENVOY OF GOD

THE 1910 revolution in Portugal which overthrew the monarchy, brought to power a clique of Marxist-leaning anarchists and freemasons whose avowed aim was to stamp out religion in that intensely Catholic country within two generations. Many prelates and priests, including the Jesuits, were driven abroad and those remaining were forbidden to wear clerical dress. The great monasteries and abbeys were converted into barracks and Government offices, the religious oath was abolished in the courts, Holy Days were secularised and marriage declared to be a mere civil contract. By 1916 the shortage of priests in the country had become acute, but in the village of Fatima, some eighteen miles south-east of the busy town of Leiria, the inhabitants still counted themselves fortunate to have a resident pastor, Fr. Emmanuel Ferreira, a devout, austere, yet rather autocratic and inflexible man. His parishioners were sturdy, hard-working peasants, many of whom owned small patches of land in the vicinity where they strove to coax grain, olives and figs from the infertile soil and graze sheep in the adjoining, rock-strewn fields.

Hard by was the tiny hamlet of Aljustrel, a loose straggle of stuccoed and white-washed stone houses twisting along a narrow lane lined with grey crumbling walls — a relatively listless place pervaded by the sound and smell of farming activity. Here lived Antonio dos Santos with his wife Maria Rosa and their six children. Though affable and popular with his neighbours, Antonio was content to leave the raising of his large family to his capable, robust wife. She worked with conscious zeal to instill the Faith in her children, adopting an affectionate but rigid strictness, backed up by the threat of a good thrashing if they were disobedient or told the slightest untruth. Their youngest child, Lucia, who was born on 22 March 1907, grew up to be a devout, loveable young girl, fond of games and immensely popular with other children in the hamlet. Up the road lived her uncle, Ti Marto, and his wife Olimpia, with their nine children, the youngest of whom were Francisco (born 11 June 1908) and Jacinta (born 11 March 1910). The former was a peaceful, tolerant, good-humoured boy, at once gentle and fearless, who thought nothing of wandering out in the surrounding wild moorland at night in search of rabbits and snakes. By contrast, his sister was a lively, capricious child, though possessed of a sweet and gentle nature with a particular fondness for lambs, which she loved to clasp to her heart in imitation of the Good Shepherd.

During the early spring of 1916, Olimpia permitted Francisco and Jacinta to accompany Lucia each day as she took her family's sheep out to pasture in the neighbouring hills, and the trio gradually developed a close friendship. One morning, while they were grazing the sheep at a favourite spot known as the Cabeco, a rocky knoll not far from the summit of a large prominence near their home, a strong wind suddenly sprang up which made them stop playing abruptly. Looking out across the distant valley, they were astonished to see a dazzling globe of light like a miniature sun, gliding slowly and majestically towards them. As it approached, the children could see the ball of light gradually resolve itself into the shape of a transparent young man of about fourteen, "more brilliant than crystal pierced by the rays of the sun," as Lucia later described him. Standing before them in supernatural radiance he said in a voice of grave beauty: "Do not be afraid. I am the Angel of Peace. Pray with me." Then kneeling down and bowing so low that his forehead touched the ground, he recited the following prayer three times in a voice that quivered with fervour: "My God, I believe, I adore, I hope, I love Thee. I ask pardon for those who do not believe, nor adore, nor hope, nor love Thee." Then rising he said, "Pray like that. The Hearts of Jesus and Mary are attentive to the voice of your supplications." Having said this, he gradually faded in the sunlit air.

The children were so overcome with the sense of the supernatural that they remained on their knees for many hours, repeating the prayer of the angel over and over again. Finally, towards evening, they recovered somewhat and trudged home weak and dazed, for the sense of the presence of God still clung to them like the aftermath of an awesome dream. It was only after some weeks that the supernatural atmosphere which enveloped them gradually faded away. It is noteworthy that Francisco heard nothing of what the angel had said; he began reciting the prayer only when he heard the other two saying it. This significant detail was repeated during the apparitions of Our Lady the following year: he only saw the vision; Jacinta both saw and heard the vision; while Lucia saw, heard and spoke to the apparition.

During the summer of that same year, while the children were resting from the heat one day under the shade of some fig trees by a well in Lucia's garden, the angel suddenly stood by them a second time. "What are you doing?" he exclaimed in a tone of gentle admonition, "you must pray. You must pray a great deal.

The Hearts of Jesus and Mary have designs of mercy on you. Offer up prayers and sacrifices constantly to the Most High." Lucia asked him how they were to make sacrifices and the angel answered: "Make everything you do a sacrifice and offer it to God in reparation for the countless sins by which He is offended and in supplication for the conversion of sinners. In this way, you will bring peace to your country. I am its Guardian Angel, the Angel of Portugal. Above all, accept and bear with submission all the sufferings which the Lord may send you."

The words of the angel illumined the souls of the three children "like a light which made us understand who and what God really is, how much He loves us and wishes to be loved," as Lucia wrote many years later. "The value of sacrifice now, for the first time, became clear to us. Suddenly we knew its appeal to God and its power to convert sinners. From that day on we began to offer to God all that mortified us, all that was difficult or unpleasant. And we also spent hour after hour, prostrate upon the ground, repeating the angel's prayer over and over again."

After the angel vanished, the children were again overwhelmed by the same profound sense of the supernatural which left them wholly absorbed in God. Francisco had to wait an entire day before Lucia could bring herself to repeat the angel's words to him. As for little Jacinta, she could only murmur: "I don't know what's wrong with me. I can't speak, nor sing, nor play. I'm not able to do anything." "Nor can I," Francisco agreed. "But what does it matter? The angel was more beautiful than anything; let's go on thinking about him."

Some three months later, while the children were grazing their sheep at the Cabeco again, the angel suddenly appeared to them a third time. Through the white radiance of his presence the children could see that he held a chalice with a Host above it, from which drops of Blood fell into the cup. Leaving these suspended in mid-air, he prostrated himself on the ground before them and repeated the following sublime prayer of reparation three times in the same tone of trembling fervour.

"Most Holy Trinity, Father, Son and Holy Spirit, I adore Thee profoundly. I offer Thee the most Precious Body, Blood, Soul and Divinity of Our Lord Jesus Christ, really and truly present in every tabernacle of the world in reparation for the countless outrages, sacrileges and indifferences by which He is offended. And through the infinite merits of the Sacred Heart of Jesus and of the Immaculate Heart of Mary, I beg Thee to convert poor sinners."

The angel then gave the Host to Lucia and the chalice to Francisco and Jacinta to drink from. He then prostrated himself once more on the ground and repeated the above prayer three times very slowly with the children before disappearing from their

ecstatic gaze. Lucia's description of this overpowering experience
and sense of utter weakness and detachment from their earthly
surroundings recalls the words of St. Paul after he had been taken
up into the Third Heaven and could only stammer that he was
unable to tell whether or not he had been completely detached
from his body. Eventually Francisco managed to say: "The angel
gave you Holy Communion, Lucia, but what was it that he gave
Jacinta and me?". "It was also Communion," Jacinta interposed.
"Didn't you see the Blood dripping from the Host?". "I knew it
was God in me," the boy admitted, "but I didn't know how it
was." Then because he could speak no more, he prostrated
himself on the ground again and remained praying with the others
until the evening shadows crept over the rocks around them. Lucia
recalled that the apparitions of Our Lady in the following year produced quite different effects in them. "We felt the same intimate
happiness, the same peace and joy, but instead of physical prostration, an expansion of movement; instead of this annihilation in the
Divine Presence, a desire to exult with joy: there was no difficulty
of speech, but rather a desire of communication. All the same, we
felt the need for silence, especially about certain things."

The apparitions of the angel were not revealed until Lucia wrote
her second Memoir in November 1937. She had earlier been forbidden by her spiritual directors to divulge the visions, presumably
to enable Our Lady's message to be more readily accepted first.
Several theologians voiced regret that these visions could not be
corroborated by a second person, but it has recently come to light
that as far back as 1921 Lucia told one of the nuns in the Asile of
Vilar the prayers of the angel, though without alluding to the
supernatural circumstances in which she had learnt them. The
visions themselves teach us the importance of remembering the
existence of angels, their mission of leading us to God, the role of
our guardian angel and the angel of our country. Later we shall
expand on the significance of the prayers taught us by the angel of
Fatima.

In the past, certain theologians have questioned several aspects
of the above apparitions. They claim that the offering of the
Divinity of Our Lord to the Holy Trinity is, at least, "an innova-
tion"; that angels cannot consecrate bread and wine into the Body
and Blood of Christ; and that "the infinite merits of the Sacred
Heart of Jesus and of the Immaculate Heart of Mary" is
"inaccurate terminology." When questioned on these supposed
difficulties, Lucia insisted that she had quoted the exact words of
the angel and she added with a wry smile: "Perhaps the angel did
not know his theology!"

In passing, critics of the above visions would do well to ponder
the fact that the Angel of Peace is one of the titles of the Arch-

angel Michael and to question his words is tantamount to questioning the wisdom of God Himself. The first objection is surprising, to say the least. Christ is always both Priest and Victim and can therefore always be offered to the Holy Trinity. As for the angel being incapable of consecrating the bread and wine into the Body and Blood of Christ, this surely could have been effected by Our Lord Himself, the High Priest.

As regards the "infinite merits of the Sacred Heart of Jesus and of the Immaculate Heart of Mary", the combined merits are certainly infinite since the part contributed by Jesus is infinite. The part contributed by Mary is, of course, finite, but is abundantly adequate for her role in distributing the graces which have their source in Jesus alone.

During the winter of 1916-17 and the following spring, the children spent much of their time together in prayer and recollected silence. As the weather grew warmer, they led their flock of sheep out further afield. On Sunday 13 May, preceding the Ascension, and which was the Feast of Our Lady of the Blessed Sacrament[1], Lucia decided to take the flock to a vast natural hollow in the ground known as the Cova da Iria, some two or three kilometres distant. A deserted road bordered by loose stone walls ran along one side of the Cova; it was so infrequently used that its surface was often overgrown with grass. A solitary inn was the only sign of habitation in a wilderness of tumbling mountains and moorland. Here and there lay irregular smallholdings, laced by a tangled network of rough stone walls marking their boundaries. The sides of the Cova descended all round in a gentle declivity to an oval-shaped floor dotted with olive and holm oak trees and criss-crossed by the characteristic stone walls dividing patches under cultivation and grassy areas reserved for the pasturing of sheep.

When the children had settled down in the Cova with their sheep and recited the rosary, they began to amuse themselves by building a little stone house round a small furze bush. Suddenly there was a vivid flash of light. They looked up, startled, into the azure sky, for there was no sign of a storm. But Lucia, being weatherwise, felt certain that one must be brewing behind the mountains and began gathering up the flock of sheep to head for home. Suddenly a second flash rivetted them in stupefaction. A few paces away on a small holm oak stood a Lady all of dazzling light. They were so close to her that they found themselves bathed in the light that radiated from her person. Their eyes smarted from the Lady's brilliance and beauty; they could perceive that she was standing on a sapling holm oak and gazing down at them with a tender regard. "She was more brilliant than the sun," Lucia later described her, "and she radiated a sparkling light from her person, clearer and more intense than that of a crystal filled with glittering water and transpierced by the rays of the most burning sun."

Enraptured, the children contemplated the apparition, drinking in the overpowering beauty of the Lady's features. "Do not be afraid," she said in a voice of gentle reassurance, "I will do you no harm."

"Where are you from?" Lucia managed to ask.

"I am from Heaven."

The children could now see that the vision wore a white mantle of immaculate purity, bordered by a stronger light, which fell to her feet. A prominent star shone from the hem of this sun-like robe, while from her hands hung a rosary of diamond-like brilliance.

"What do you want of us?" Lucia asked at length.

"I came to ask you to come here on the thirteenth day for six months at this same time, and then I will tell you who I am and what I want. And afterwards, I will return here a seventh time."

Gaining confidence Lucia asked: "Will I go to Heaven?"

"Yes you will."

"And Jacinta?"

"She also."

"And Francisco? Will he go to Heaven too?"

The Lady paused and looked at Francisco. Then she said: "Yes. But first, he must say many rosaries."

Lucia then asked about the fate of two girls of Aljustrel who had recently died and the Lady replied that one was already in Heaven and the other would be "in Purgatory until the end of the world." She then asked: "Would you like to offer yourselves to God, to accept all the sufferings which He may send you in reparation for the countless sins by which He is offended and in supplication for the conversion of sinners?"

Lucia consented, speaking for all three. The Lady nodded her approval and said: "Then you will have much to suffer, but the grace of God will be your comfort."

As she said these words, she opened her hands and streams of intense light flowed from them which overwhelmed the childrens' souls, causing them to feel "lost in God" Whom they recognised in that light. By an interior impulse they threw themselves to the ground and cried out with passionate fervour: "O Most Holy Trinity I adore Thee! My God, my God, I love Thee in the Most Blessed Sacrament!"

The Lady waited for them to finish and then asked them to recite the rosary every day. With that she rose in a cloud of light and glided serenely away into the eastern sky.

It should be mentioned in passing that her promise to return to the Cova da Iria a seventh time, which many believe is yet to come, is now known to have already occurred. She appeared to Lucia there as the child was leaving for a boarding school in Oporto a few years later and gave her a private message of reassurance in anticipation of the difficulties she was soon to encounter.

Also Our Lady's statement that one of the deceased girls of Aljustrel "will be in Purgatory until the end of the world," must be interpreted conditionally: that is, she will remain there unless satisfaction is made for her on earth by Masses and prayers. (cf. the Book of Jonas; Exodus 32: 10-14; and Jer. 18: 7-8).

Lucia cautioned her cousins to say nothing of what they had seen for fear of disbelief, but Jacinta's heart was too full. Francisco was also overcome. "We were on fire in that light that was God, and yet we were not burnt," he exclaimed. "How wonderful God is! How can we ever describe Him! It would be impossible! And yet . . . He looked so sad. If only I could console Him."

Predictably Jacinta told her parents what they had seen and there was a general reaction of disbelief; only Ti Marto decided to reserve his judgement. Next morning the news jolted the sleepy village; Lucia's mother was convinced that her child was lying and punished her daughter repeatedly when she refused to deny her story. The children also suffered from the disbelief of neighbours; they were ridiculed and even spat upon. Remembering how the Lady had warned them that they would have much to suffer, they sought refuge in each others' company, spending long hours in prayer and practicing many sacrifices. On the morning of 13 June, only a few dozen curious people decided to accompany them to the Cova da Iria. One of them was Maria Carreira who became the first custodian of the shrine.

Precisely at noon the Lady in light appeared above the holm oak again and though she was invisible to the onlookers, everyone saw what seemed to be a small white cloud of light float down from the eastern sky and hover over the little tree where the children were kneeling in ecstasy.

"My Lady," Lucia began in a tremulous voice, "what do you want of me?"

"I want you to come here on the thirteenth day of next month and to pray the rosary every day and I want you to learn to read."

Lucia asked for the cure of a sick person and the Lady said: "If she is converted, she will be cured within a year."

"I want you to take us to Heaven," Lucia said with childish simplicity.

"Yes," the Lady replied, "I will take Francisco and Jacinta soon, but you must remain on earth for some time. Jesus wishes to use you to make me better known and loved. He wishes to establish in the world devotion to my Immaculate Heart."

Lucia was suddenly sad. "Must I stay here all alone?"

"No, my child," the Lady replied gently. "And would that make you suffer? Do not be disheartened. My Immaculate Heart will never abandon you, but will be your refuge and the way that will lead you to God."

As she said these words, the Lady again opened her hands on the three children and communicated to them the same immense light that had overwhelmed them a month earlier. Francisco and Jacinta seemed to be in that part of the light which rose towards Heaven and Lucia in the rays which spread over the world. In the palm of the Lady's right hand, the children could see a Heart, ringed by thorns which seemed to pierce it. They understood this to be the Immaculate Heart of Mary, grieved by the sins of humanity and seeking reparation.

As the Lady rose into the sky, Lucia stood up and cried: "Look! There she goes!" Maria Carreira later testified that they heard "a sound like a rocket a long way off." The bystanders could see the little cloud of light drift away into the eastern sky. Then they noticed that the leaves of the holm oak were bent in the direction that the Lady had taken as if her garments had trailed across them. They remained like that for some hours and only gradually regained their normal position.

Back home the children were subjected to a milder chorus of disbelief, for word had spread that there might be something in their story after all. But Lucia's mother refused to even consider that Our Lady was appearing to the likes of her daughter and virtually persecuted her for failing to retract her story. Finally the parish priest intervened and after questioning the children closely, came to the conclusion that the visions might be the work of the devil. The notion appalled Lucia; she resolved there and then to keep well away from the Cova da Iria in future. Her cousins pleaded with her to change her mind. "The devil? Not at all," Jacinta insisted. "They say he is very, very ugly and he lives in Hell. That Lady was so beautiful! And we saw her going up to Heaven." But Lucia remained adamant. The pastor's warning loomed large in her young mind and seemed to be reinforced by a terrifying dream of the devil that she had one night. After that she lost her inclination for sacrifices and began to avoid the company of her cousins. She felt she didn't want to see either them or the Cova da Iria ever again.

NOTES

1. On 30 December 1905, Pope St. Pius X wrote the following prayer in his own hand: "Domina nostra Sanctissimi Sacramenti, ora pro nobis" (Our Lady of the Most Blessed Sacrament, pray for us). Shortly after, the Holy See granted permission for the celebration of a feast in honour of Our Lady of the Most Blessed Sacrament for 13 May. cf. *Our Lady of the Most Blessed Sacrament,* Sentinel Press, New York, p. v. This invaluable book contains the writings of St. Peter Julian Eymard on the subject.

III

HELL AND THE PROPHECIES

LATE on the morning of 13 July, Lucia felt a sudden impulse to go to the Cova da Iria again. Hurrying across to her cousins' house, she found them kneeling in tears, praying their rosary.

"Haven't you gone yet?" she exclaimed. "It is almost midday already."

Jacinta looked up brokenly. "We didn't dare go without you," she sobbed.

"Well, I've changed my mind," Lucia rejoined. "Come on, let's go together."

Overjoyed at this unexpected news, Francisco and Jacinta sprang to their feet and, followed by Ti Marto and Olimpia, made their way along the twisting road out of Aljustrel towards the Cova da Iria, surrounded by growing numbers of devout and curious spectators. Some 5,000 people had crowded around the holm oak that morning and two powerfully-built men made an opening in the throng for the children to pass through, and then protected them from being crushed. On reaching the little tree, the children fell to their knees and began reciting the rosary. Minutes later Lucia cried out: "Shut your umbrellas, the Lady is coming!" The people duly obeyed and waited in tense silence as the fiery sun beat down on their unprotected heads.

All at once, a little white cloud could be seen floating down from the eastern sky and coming to rest on the holm oak. Everyone present was conscious of a sudden cooling of the air and a lessening of the sun's light. Ti Marto, who was standing close to Lucia, became aware of a sound "like the buzzing of a horse-fly in a bottle."

"What do you want of me," Lucia asked, now in ecstasy.

And the Lady answered: "I want you to come here on the thirteenth day of next month and to continue to pray the rosary every day in honour of Our Lady of the Rosary, in order to obtain peace for the world and the end of the war, for she alone can help."

"I would like to ask who you are," Lucia said, "and to perform a miracle so that people will believe that you are appearing to us."

"Continue to come here every month," the Lady replied. "In October I will tell you who I am and what I want. And I will perform a miracle so that everyone may see and believe."

Lucia then presented some petitions that had been entrusted to her — the cure of a cripple, the conversion of a family in Fatima, and to take to Heaven a certain sick person. The Lady answered that she would not cure the cripple, but would give him a livelihood if he recited the rosary every day (he became sacristan at the shrine for many years); that the family in Fatima would be converted in the following year if the persons pleading for them recited the daily rosary; and that the sick person should not be impatient to die soon "since I know very well when I will come to take her." At this point, Lucia was heard to say aloud: "Yes, she wants people to recite the rosary. People must recite the rosary."

The Lady's face then grew very grave and she said: "Sacrifice yourselves for sinners and say often, especially when you make some sacrifice: O my Jesus, this is for love of You, for the conversion of sinners, and in reparation for the offences committed against the Immaculate Heart of Mary." At these words, she opened her hands on the three children once again and the light streaming from them seemed to penetrate the earth and the children beheld a vision of Hell. Lucia cried out in terror, calling upon Our Lady. "We could see a vast sea of fire," she revealed many years later. "Plunged in the flames were demons and lost souls, as if they were red-hot coals, transparent and black or bronze-coloured, in human form, which floated about in the conflagration, borne by the flames which issued from them, with clouds of smoke falling on all sides as sparks fall in a great conflagration without weight or equilibrium, amid shrieks and groans of sorrow and despair that horrified us and caused us to tremble with fear. The devils could be distinguished by horrible and loathesome forms of animals, frightful and unknown, but transparent like black coals that have turned red-hot."[1]

Full of fear, the children raised their eyes beseechingly to the Lady who said to them with unspeakable sadness and tenderness: "You saw Hell where the souls of poor sinners go. In order to save them, God wishes to establish in the world devotion to my Immaculate Heart. If people do what I ask, many souls will be saved and there will be peace. The war is going to end. But if people do not stop offending God, another, even worse, will begin in the reign of Pius XI. When you see a night illuminated by an unknown light, know that it is the great sign that God gives you that He is going to punish the world by means of war, hunger and persecution of the Church and of the Holy Father. To prevent it, I shall come to ask for the consecration of Russia to my Immaculate Heart and the Communion of reparation on the first Saturdays. If people attend to my requests, Russia will be converted and the world will have peace. If not, Russia will spread its errors throughout the world, fomenting wars and persecutions of the

Church. The good will be martyred, the Holy Father will have much to suffer, and various nations will be annihilated. In the end, my Immaculate Heart will triumph. The Holy Father will consecrate Russia to me; it will be converted, and a certain period of peace will be granted to the world. In Portugal, the dogmas of the Faith will always be kept . . . *(Here follows the third secret which has never been revealed).*[2] Do not tell this to anyone. Francisco — yes, you may tell him. When you say the rosary, say after each mystery: O my Jesus, forgive us our sins, save us from the fires of Hell and lead all souls to Heaven, especially those most in need."

There was a pause and then Lucia said: "Do you want anything more of me?"

"No," the Lady replied. "Today, I want nothing else of you."

At this moment Ti Marto recalled: "There was a sort of thunderclap and the little arch which had been put up over the holm oak to hang lanterns on shook as if in an earthquake. Lucia got up off her knees so quickly that her skirts blew out all round her, and pointing to the sky she cried: 'There she goes! There she goes!' And then: 'Now you can't see her any more.' And this too was for me a great proof. The little cloud over the tree melted away."

Immediately the children were surrounded by demanding spectators. "What did the Lady say to you? Why did you go so white? Why did you cry out in fear? What happened?"

Lucia could only say: "It's a secret."

"Is it a good one?"

"Good for some, but bad for others."

The pressure of the crowd increased and Ti Marto, fearing that the children would be suffocated, lifted Jacinta under his arm and covering her face with his hat, elbowed his way through the throng and scrambled up the grassy slope of the Cova to the relative safety of the road. Behind him, two other men carried Lucia and Francisco. The sun beat down fiercely on the unshaded road and Lucia mustered her remaining energy to announce to the crowd that the Lady had promised a miracle for the 13th of October to prove the reality of her appearances. The news only heightened the excitement of the crowd already animated by the heavenly signs just seen and seething with speculation about the secret. Word of the promised miracle and the secret flew across Portugal and generated intense interest and debate. The apparitions were now the talking point of the country.

At this stage, it is necessary to make a brief digression and examine the importance and significance of the foregoing vision to our world today. In retrospect, we can perceive that the vision of Hell was particularly intended for our age when many Christians play down the concept of eternal punishment or deny its very existence And in the secular world, even the meaning of sin is fast being lost: jurists, for example, have turned it into a crime, while psychiatrists have labelled it a complex. The rejection of sin has resulted in the loss of guilt; much of today's evil is perpetrated without thought of repentance. The philosopher Max Scheler recently drew attention to this pernicious development and to the fact that while sin multiplies everywhere, the sense of guilt correspondingly diminishes.

Nor is this all. Inside the Church, many liberal theologians regard the doctrine of Hell as being unsuitable for the mentality of modern man and are infecting others with this view. They are quick to admit God's love and mercy, but not His justice. And they maintain this one-footed stance despite the fact that in the gospels, Our Lord stressed the existence of Hell fifteen times. Pope Paul VI reiterated this teaching in his *Credo of the People of God:* those who refuse God's love and mercy to the end "will go to the fire that will never be extinguished." It is, perhaps, significant that sermons on Hell are less frequently heard and confessionals are emptying at a time when sin is abounding as never before. On all sides we are assailed by glaring sex, brutal violence, abortion-on-demand, drug addiction, blasphemy, theft, divorce, infidelity, pre-marital experiences, pornography, rape, prostitution and brazen scandal in the media. A single immoral TV programme can be the occasion for millions of sins against the sixth Commandment. As Cardinal Hoeffner of Cologne stated at Fatima on 13 October 1977: "Today, we are witnessing a great rebellion against the holy will of God. Moral behaviour has deteriorated to such a degree that it could not be imagined twenty years ago . . ."

Explaining this disastrous trend, the Bishop of Fatima stated at Pontevedra on 10 December 1975:

"In the light of the Fatima message, sin is not a phenomena of the sociological order, but is, in the true theological concept, an offence against God with necessary social consequences. Perhaps no other century as the century we live in has had a life so sinful. But there is something new added in the sins of this century: the man of today, more sinful than those who came before him, has lost the sense of sin. He sins, but laughs and even boasts of his sin . . . Man of today has arrived at this stage because he has placed a division between himself and God . . . believing that when God is ignored, everything is possible. The man of this century wishes to realise himself as stronger than God and against God, and comes finally to the point of being man debased, anti-man, because man can only perfectly realise himself in God."

It was in anticipation of this global insurrection against God that the Blessed Virgin interceded with her Divine Son to permit the frightening reality of Hell to be shown to the world for a searing instant. We read in the parable of Dives and Lazarus that God refused to show Hell to the world, explaining that its existence must be accepted through Faith. That Our Lady obtained the grace of this vision seems like the action of a broken-hearted Mother seeing great numbers of her children in dire peril of being cast into eternal fire.

This view was reinforced by an interview with Lucia in 1953 given to the great Jesuit apostle of the mercy of God, Fr. Lombardi, which was afterwards recorded in the Vatican weekly *Osservatore della Domenica* of 7 February 1954.

"Tell me," said Fr. Lombardi, "is the Better World movement a response of the Church to the words spoken by Our Lady?"

"Father," Lucia replied, "there is certainly a great need for this renewal. If it is not done, and taking into account the present development of humanity, only a limited number of the human race will be saved."

"Do you really believe that many will go to Hell?" Fr. Lombardi asked. "I hope that God will save the greater part of humanity." (He had just written a book entitled: *Salvation for those without faith.*)

"Father, many will be lost."

"It is true that the world is full of evil, but there is always a hope of salvation."

"No Father, many will be lost."

Fr. Lombardi remembered that Lucia had seen Hell and added: "Her words disturbed me. I returned to Italy with that grave warning impressed on my heart." The good priest had, perhaps, overlooked the fact that little Jacinta had also spoken of "many, many souls" being lost.

It is not our purpose here to recount the theology of the doctrine of Hell, but only to explain *why* Our Lady showed the vision at the beginning of our sin-drenched century. Not only was it intended to confirm the essential doctrine and powerfully influence us to stop offending God, but it was also meant to stimulate in us a greater devotion to the Immaculate Heart of Mary as the special means given by God to draw men away from sin.

The vision of Hell had the greatest impact on little Jacinta. She became obsessed with the sight of those red, raging flames and the terrifying sight and sound of millions of screaming demons and lost souls. "Oh Hell! Oh Hell!" she would wail, wringing her hands impotently. "Mother of God have pity on those who do not amend their lives." "If men only knew what awaits them in eternity, they would do everything in their power to change their lives." Frequently, she would call to her brother saying: "Francisco, are you praying with me? We must pray very much to save souls from Hell.

So many go there. So many." At other times she would ask Lucia: "Why doesn't Our Lady show Hell to sinners? If only they saw it, they would never commit sins again." On one occasion she said to Lucia: "Look, I am going to Heaven soon, but you are to stay here. If Our Lady lets you, tell everyone what Hell is like so that they won't sin anymore and not go there."

The three children undertook the most severe penances for the salvation of sinners. They wore a rope tightly round their waists; they gave their lunches to the poor, or even to their sheep; they didn't drink during the furnace-like heat of August 1917 — an almost unendurable penance as anyone who has stayed in Fatima during that month will appreciate. Later, Jacinta even wanted to drink water from a pond frequented by cattle. However imprudent this would be, the thought of Hell dominated every consideration of hygiene, discomfort or pain.

In the light of these and other heroic penances practiced by the children, it is not difficult to see why Our Lady requested that the revelation of Hell be kept a secret. Had it been divulged in 1917, no one would have believed it. In the parable of Dives and Lazarus, Our Lord stated that even if someone returned from the dead to warn of Hell, no one would pay any attention. When Lucia was finally permitted to reveal the vision in 1941, the extraordinary penances of the three children had become known, making belief in the revelation credible.

To the necessity of penance for sinners must also be joined that of prayer. Our Lady constantly reminded the children to pray a great deal and they readily responded by spending long hours on their knees under a blistering sun, reciting the rosary and the Angel's prayer over and over again. Recently, Lucia, who is now a Carmelite nun in Coimbra, stressed the imperative need of prayer to counter the flood of evil today. In a letter to a nephew (who is a Salesian priest) she wrote: "It is sad that so many are allowing themselves to be dominated by the diabolical wave that is sweeping the world and they are so blind that they cannot see their error. Their principle mistake is that they have abandoned prayer . . . What I recommend to you above all is that you get close to the tabernacle and pray. In fervent prayer you receive the light, strength and grace that you need to sustain you . . . In prayer, you will find more science, more light, more strength, more grace and virtue than you could ever achieve by reading many books or by great studies . . . Never consider the time wasted that you spend in prayer. You will discover that in prayer, God communicates to you the light, strength and grace you need to do all He expects of you . . . We all need to intensify our life of intimate union with God and this we can only attain through prayer . . . Let time be lacking for everything else, but never for prayer . . . The principal

cause of evil in the world and the falling away of so many consecrated souls is the lack of union with God in prayer. If we are not
careful and attentive in obtaining the strength from God, we will
fail because our times are very bad and we are weak. Only God's
strength can sustain us."[3]

Immediately after the vision of Hell and Our Lady's appeal for
devotion to her Immaculate Heart, she outlined the future facing
mankind if her requests were accepted, and alternatively, if they
were rejected. The prophecy, as we have seen, is fairly lengthy and
in the past gave rise to several difficulties which, to a certain
extent, impeded the spread of the message. One of the chief
reasons for this misunderstanding was the desire to relate the
prophecy to current world events when it required the perspective of subsequent developments for it to be seen in a clearer light.
It was argued that the Second World War started in the reign of
Pius XII, not Pius XI; that it was primarily caused by Nazi
Germany, not Soviet Russia; and that the latter country was consecrated to the Immaculate Heart of Mary by Pius XII on 7 July
1952 and remains unconverted.[4]

Lucia was questioned about the first difficulty and insisted that
Our Lady had mentioned Pius XI by name. She added that the
Second World War actually began with the invasion of Austria and
the Anschluss in 1938 and that Pius XI had stated as much. The
latter died on 10 February 1939 so that Pius XII was on the papal
throne when Poland was invaded on 1 September 1939 and Britain
and France declared war on Germany a few days later. However,
it is just possible that Lucia was merely expressing her private
opinion regarding the start of the Second World War.

If this view is correct (it is purely a personal one), then it is
probable that Our Lady was referring to two separate punish-
ments, the first beginning in the reign of Pius XI (which was the
Spanish Civil War) and the second, preceded by an "unknown
light", to follow later. Our Lady had said that the first punishment
would be "even worse" than the First World War and certainly the
Spanish Civil War was incomparably worse, being essentially a war
against God in which untold numbers of churches were destroyed, and 14 bishops and 7,000 priests and religious were martyred. The anti-God nature of the conflict was epitomised by the
'execution' by a firing squad of the famous granite statue of the
Sacred Heart in the geographical centre of Spain.

The "unknown light" which was to be the "great sign" given by
God that the punishment of the world was at hand, occurred on
the night of 25-26 January 1938. It appeared as a vast and terrifying display of the Aurora Borealis which was seen all over the
northern hemisphere and struck fear into the hearts of millions,
many of whom believed it to be the end of the world. Newspapers

gave the event extensive coverage; the *New York Times* accorded it almost an entire page. Scientists have since tried to explain the Aurora as a natural, if rather impressive display, but Lucia has stated that had they investigated closer, they would have discovered that it could not have had a natural origin.[5] Be that as it may, the light was primarily intended as a sign to Lucia of the imminence of a global chastisement. She then wrote to the Cardinal Patriarch of Lisbon to this effect: "War is imminent. The sins of men will be washed in their own blood. Those nations will suffer most in the war which tried to destroy the Kingdom of God. Portugal will suffer some of the consequences of the war, but because of our country's consecration to the Immaculate Heart, she will not suffer them all."

Passing on to the assertion that the war which began in 1939 was primarily Hitler's war and not Soviet Russia's, it is important to remember Our Lady's exact words. "When you see a night illuminated by an unknown light, know that it is the great sign that God gives you that He is going to punish the world by means of war, hunger and persecution of the Church and of the Holy Father. To prevent it, I shall come to ask for the consecration of Russia to my Immaculate Heart and the Communion of reparation on the First Saturdays. If people attend to my requests, Russia will be converted and the world will have peace. If not, Russia will spread its errors throughout the world, fomenting wars and persecutions of the Church. The good will be martyred, the Holy Father will have much to suffer and various nations will be annihilated . . ."

From the perspective of the 1980s we can now see that Our Lady was referring to a prolonged punishment of the world, beginning in 1939 and proceeding with the spread of Communism, even to the annihilation of entire nations. The Second World War has never officially ended since no peace treaty has been signed. On the contrary, fighting with Communism began even before the capitulation of Germany (in Greece) and has since extended all over the world, resulting in literally hundreds of smaller wars, revolutions and violent persecutions of the Church.

The role of Nazi Germany accordingly marked the first ferocious chapter in this extended conflict, the dominant feature of which was the unchaining of the Soviet colossus, which has since scourged almost half the world and menaces the remaining half with an immense arsenal of thermonuclear weaponry. Hence the words of Our Lady, "to prevent it (i.e. this long conflict) I shall come to ask for the consecration of Russia . . .", could not have been more relevant. Speaking in 1917, the Queen of Prophets was looking far ahead through all the violent upheavals that have ensued since 1939 and may yet ensue, right up to the day of Russia's conversion.

NOTES

1. Since neither souls nor demons have shapes, we can assume that the imagery presented to the children was of a nature consonant with the traditional human conception of Hell.

2. It is beyond the scope of this book to discuss the Third Secret of Fatima. The full story has been recounted in an excellent book by Dr. M. Alonso, C.M.F., entitled *The Secret of Fatima: Fact and Legend,* published in 1979 by the Ravengate Press, Cambridge, USA. Dr. Alonso stresses the damage that can be done to true revelations such as La Salette, Lourdes and Fatima by the propagation of unfounded visions and messages by spurious seers — a phenomenon widely prevalent today.

3. cf. *Soul* magazine, Nov.-Dec. 1976.

4. The subject of the consecration is dealt with fully in Chapter 8.

5. Recently scientific investigation into the great aurora of 25 January 1938 tends to confirm Lucia's assertion. Auroras are associated with sunspot activity; they occur most frequently at or near maximum sunspot activity and less frequently at or near minimum sunspot activity. Yet at the time of the great aurora of 25 January 1938, there was no sunspot activity whatsoever. According to Dr. Carl Stoermer of the Institute of Theoretical Astrophysics in Oslo in a report published in the scientific journal *Die Naturwissenschaften* (26, (30)), 8 September 1938, pp. 633-38, the great aurora covered an almost unbelievable area of 500,000 square km with a vertical extent of approximately 400 km. Some of the rays reached the fantastic altitude of 700 km, which is at least 400 km beyond the height of most large auroras. It was accompanied by a strange noise "similar to the sound of burning grass and brush," reported Dr. Stoermer. Millions of people in many countries feared the world was on fire and about to end — a virtual repetition of what happened during the fall of the sun at Fatima on 13 October 1917. (see page 64).

IV

TOWARDS THE CLIMAX

SINCE all that the three children had said of the foregoing revelation concerned the need for sacrifice and the daily rosary, no one in the Cova da Iria on that torrid July afternoon could have remotely imagined what had actually transpired. But speculation was intense and as news of the apparitions spread throughout the country, hordes of inquisitive people came flocking to Aljustrel to question the little seers and if possible, to pry the secret from them. The children did their utmost to evade the endless importunity of these strangers. At the first sign of their approach, Lucia would dive under a bed, Francisco would scramble into an attic, while Jacinta simply disappeared into the nearest hiding place. If they were discovered, they would remain as taciturn as good manners required, stubbornly resisting bribes of money or sweets in exchange for the secret. While Fr. Ferreira remained coldly aloof, growing crowds thronged through the village and the Cova da Iria, trampling down the vegetables in the smallholding there owned by Lucia's father.

This development only heightened the persecution to which the child was subjected after 13 July. Her mother continued to beat her for telling such outrageous lies while her sisters tormented her for attracting swarms of strangers into the home, disrupting their sewing and weaving from which they earned much-needed money. Francisco and Jacinta fared somewhat better than their suffering cousin since Ti Marto was now a firm believer in the apparitions, though Olimpia was still sceptical. On one occasion she slapped Jacinta saying testily: "They all go to the Cova da Iria because of you." Sobbing, the child replied: "We don't ask them to go. If they want to go, they go. If not, they can stay at home."

The Church adopted an attitude of extreme reserve, partly on account of the persecution it was already suffering in the country and the fear that it would intensify if the clergy were seen to be countenancing the events of Fatima in any way. But the commotion in Aljustrel was beginning to cause concern to the Government in Lisbon. The Civic Administrator of the district of Fatima, a hated young despot named Arturo Santos, was infuriated to learn that all his efforts to stamp out religion in the region were being frustrated by three illiterate peasant children. And to cap it all, they had predicted that a public miracle would take place at noon on October 13 . . . Something drastic would have to be done if this dangerous nonsense was not to get out of hand.

He summoned the children and their parents before him at the town hall in Ourém, some nine miles distant. Ti Marto went with Lucia and her father "since it's over three leagues to Ourém and the children can't walk all that way and they aren't used to the donkey," he said flatly. The sun beat down like a furnace as the little party trundled down the steeply-winding road from Aljustrel, past plunging pine groves and crumbling stone buildings, until the dusty town of Ourém was reached shortly before noon. Here Lucia dismounted from the donkey and rubbed her bruises, for she had fallen off the animal three times on the way.

They found the town hall shut and the empty square sizzling in the midday heat. Eventually they were directed to the Administrator's office a few streets away. As they entered his room Santos gave vent to his ire and tried to frighten Lucia into revealing the secret, even threatening to kill her if she refused to tell him. The child remained silent and clung tighter to her father's hand. He threw it down with a sigh of exasperation since he had little patience with his trouble-making daughter. On being questioned, Ti Marto stoutly admitted his belief in the apparitions, evoking a growl of anger from Santos and a roar of ribald laughter from his lackeys standing in the background.

The inconclusive meeting left Santos frustrated and fuming at the realisation that a 10-year-old girl with no education had so easily thwarted him and got away with it. Late on the morning of 13 August, he suddenly materialised in the doorway of Ti Marto's home and requested to take the children in his carriage to the Cova da Iria "since I am a doubting Thomas, you know, and I must see this Lady myself before I can believe." The three children naturally shrank at the prospect of going with the Administrator and maintained that they were quite capable of walking to the Cova on their own. But Santos vehemently insisted and finally they agreed to accompany him.

As they drove off, he suddenly ordered the driver to turn away and head for Ourém. The children cried out that they were going the wrong way, but Santos threw a thick tarpaulin over them to conceal their cries and their identity from the crowds flocking to Fatima. The carriage pulled up outside Santos's house where he locked them in a room, shouting that they would not come out again until they had told him the secret. "If they kill us," Jacinta sobbed, "we will go straight to Heaven."

Meanwhile a crowd of almost 15,000 had assembled in the Cova da Iria, when suddenly word went round that the children had been kidnapped. There was a violent surge of anger which might have developed into a riot had it not been interrupted by a colossal thunder clap "that seemed like the end of the world" according to an eyewitness. This was followed by a blinding flash of light — the opposite to what might have been expected from a natural phenomenon. Everyone present could then see a little white cloud, brilliant and filmy, floating gently down from the eastern sky and coming to rest on the little holm oak where the children had knelt in previous months. Maria de Carreira has left us a graphic description of this event.

"I was not afraid. I knew there was nothing evil about the apparitions because if there were, the people would not be praying at the Cova. My constant prayer as I walked along was: 'May Our Lady guide me according to God's holy Will.' The crowd at the Cova on 13 August was even larger than in July. About eleven o'clock, Lucia's sister, Maria dos Anjos, came with some candles to light to Our Lady. The people prayed and sang religious hymns around the holm oak. The absence of the children made them very restless. When it became known that the magistrate had kidnapped them, a terrible resentment went through the crowd. There is no telling what it might have turned into, had it not thundered just then. Some thought the thunder came from the road; others thought it came from the holm oak; but it seemed to me that it came from a distance. It frightened us all and many began to cry, fearing they were going to be killed. Of course no one was killed.

"Right after the thunder came a flash, and immediately, we all noticed a little cloud, very white, beautiful and bright, that came and stayed over the holm oak. It remained a few minutes, then rose towards the heavens where it disappeared. Looking about, we noticed a strange sight that we had already seen and would see again. Everyone's face glowed rose, red, blue — all the colours of the rainbow. The trees seemed to have no branches or leaves, but were all covered with flowers; every leaf was a flower. The ground was in little squares, each one a different colour. Our clothes seemed to be transformed also into the colours of the rainbow. The two vigil lanterns hanging from the arch over the holy spot appeared to be of gold.*"

This sudden intervention of the supernatural had a mollifying effect on the crowd, but when it was all over, some of the people resolved to settle things with the Administrator and Fr. Ferreira (for many were convinced that the priest had played a part in the kidnapping). The priest was, by now, thoroughly alarmed at the course of events and after insisting vehemently that he was innocent, wrote a long letter to the Lisbon newspaper *Ordem* in which he denied any part in "this infamous and insidious

*The arch had been erected by a pious family to mark the spot of the apparitions.

calumny". He added significantly: "Thousands of eye-witnesses can attest that the presence of the children was not necessary for the Queen of Heaven to manifest her power. They will witness to the extraordinary phenomena which occurred to confirm their faith. By now it is not a trio of children, but thousands of all ages and conditions who have seen for themselves. If my absence from the Cova gave offence to believers, my presence would have been no less objectionable to unbelievers. The Blessed Virgin has no need of the parish priest in order to manifest her goodness." Clearly his abrupt change of attitude was due to the flood of favourable reports that had come to him from the Cova — that, and his fear of the people.

Meanwhile the Administrator vainly tried every trick he knew to wrest the secret from the children. They were then thrown into the public gaol and warned that a horrible death awaited them. Jacinta wept bitterly at the thought of not seeing her mother again but quietened down when Lucia suggested that she offer it up as a sacrifice. Eventually she withdrew a medal from around her neck and, hanging it on a nail on the wall, knelt down with her companions to recite the rosary. The other prisoners watched, nonplussed, but eventually joined in until they were interrupted by a guard who growled that a vat of boiling oil was now ready for them if they didn't reveal the secret. They were then marched off to Santos's office and given a final chance. They refused. As Jacinta was dragged from the room, Francisco recited a Hail Mary on his rosary. The Administrator asked what he was doing. "I am saying a Hail Mary so that Jacinta may not be afraid," the lad said tightly. The door opened and a guard announced that Jacinta was dead. Francisco was threatened next, but he too shook his head and was half carried out of the room. Lucia was now all alone with Santos. The man's stature seemed to grow like an ogre as he roared at her to reveal the secret, or suffer an agonising death. Stiff with fear, she managed a brief shake of her head and was promptly dragged outside. "I fully expected to be boiled alive," she told John Haffert years later. Apparently, her terror was so great that it overlayed Our Lady's words to her on 13 June that she would have to remain some time in the world. A few moments later to her inexpressible relief, she found herself alive and safe with her companions in an adjoining room. Later that afternoon, the exasperated Administrator finally gave up and drove the children back to the Fatima rectory.

It was the feast of the Assumption and the people were just emerging from Mass when the children were suddenly seen outside the priest's house. Ti Marto swept Jacinta up in his arms: a crowd quickly gathered round demanding the whereabouts of Santos. When he appeared, a near-riot ensued and had it not been for the prompt action of Ti Marto in quietening the mob, the Administrator might have been lynched. But this despicable episode was to have a far more serious consequence.

On the afternoon of Sunday 19 August, Lucia, Francisco and his brother John were pasturing the sheep in a rocky field known as Valinhos, about a mile from Fatima, when suddenly they noticed the beginning of the extraordinary atmospheric phenomena that had preceded the visions in the Cova da Iria. There was a sudden flash of light and Lucia, realising that Our Lady must be coming, beseeched John to run off for Jacinta. The boy refused, saying that he too wanted to see the beautiful Lady. Lucia was at her wits end; finally she succeeded in sending John back by pressing two small coins into his hand and promising more when he returned with his sister. At Jacinta's arrival there was a second flash and the three children saw the Lady in light standing on a nearby tree, though John saw nothing.

The Lady urged the children to continue going to the Cova da Iria on the thirteenth of the month and to pray the rosary every day. She repeated her promise to perform a miracle on 13 October. "Pray, pray a great deal and make many sacrifices," she said with a tender earnestness, "for many souls go to Hell because they have no one to make sacrifices and to pray for them." She complained about the ill treatment to which the children had been subjected and said that on account of this, the miracle intended for October would be "less great". And here we have one of the most solemn lessons in the entire story of Fatima. How great would the miracle have been if the children had not been kidnapped? Would it have been of longer duration? Would it have been seen all over Portugal? Perhaps over Spain or even France, bringing incalculable benefits to the Fatima apostolate and the cause of world peace? We shall never know. All we do know is that the actions of one evil man, Arturo Santos, have endangered the lives of everyone living today. And this underlines a deep truth, frequently ignored today. Each sin committed in the world adversely affects everyone else, just as each merit gained favourably affects all others. We shall be examining the theological basis and implications of this truth in a later chapter.

Our Lady then added that in October, "St. Joseph too will come with the Holy Child to bring peace to the world. Our Lord will also come to bless the people. Our Lady of the Rosary and Our Lady of Sorrows will come too." Shortly afterwards the vision rose in a cloud of light and quickly disappeared. The children noticed that the branches of the tree on which she stood exuded a delicious fragrance. They broke off some sprays and hurried back to the village. Jacinta explained what had just happened to Lucia's mother who remained incredulous until pressed to smell the foliage that Jacinta held out to her. The sudden awareness of the incredibly beautiful fragrance jolted Maria Rosa; for the first time she began to wonder if there was not some truth in the childrens' story after all.

News of the celestial phenomena witnessed by thousands of impartial observers during the August apparition and the subsequent reaction of the secular authorities combined to attract an immense multitude to the Cova da Iria for the 13th September. Among them were a number of priests for the first time, including Mgr. J. Quaresma, Vicar General of Leiria, and Canon Formigão, professor of theology at the seminary in Santarém. "From the previous evening," wrote an eyewitness, "I saw the endless stream of people coming from a distance on foot to Fatima in order to see the apparition . . . I was deeply moved and more than once tears came to my eyes on seeing the piety, the prayers and the ardent faith of the many thousands of pilgrims who recited the rosary on the way . . ."

At midday the sun began to lose its brightness until the vast crowd could see the stars shining as on 13 July. Wrote Mgr. Quaresma later: "The crowd prays all the time . . . Suddenly cries of surprise and joy are heard. Thousands of arms are raised towards a point in the sky. 'Look, there she is!' 'She is here, down there!' 'Do you see?' In the sky there is not a single cloud. I raise my eyes and begin to examine the sky more closely. My companion says with a tinge of malice: 'There! You are beginning to look, too!' To my surprise, I see clearly and distinctly, a globe of light advancing from east to west, gliding slowly and majestically through the air. My friend looks also, and he has the good fortune to see the same unexpected vision. Suddenly the globe with its extraordinary light vanished, but near us a little girl of about ten continues to cry joyfully: 'I still see it! I still see it! Now it is going down!' 'What do you think of this globe?' I ask my friend. 'I believe it is the Blessed Virgin,' he answers without hesitation. This was also my conviction. The children contemplated the Mother of God in person, while to us was granted the grace of seeing the vehicle (if one may so express it) which conveyed her."

As the crowd strained forward, they could see a little white cloud settle over the holm oak where the three children were now kneeling in ecstasy. Then suddenly there was a rain of colourful "rose petals" which vanished on reaching the ground. Lucia was heard to cry out: "You must pray!" Recalls an eyewitness: "Never will I forget the deep impression made on me by the sight of all these thousands of pilgrims falling on their knees at the voice of a child of ten, and in tears praying and imploring with confidence the maternal protection of the Queen of Heaven."

"What do you want of me?" Lucia asked the vision.

"Continue to pray the rosary every day in order to obtain the end of the war. In October Our Lord will also come, and Our Lady of Sorrows and of Mount Carmel and St. Joseph with the Child Jesus, to bless the world." She added: "God is pleased with your sacrifices, but He does not want you to sleep with the rope on; wear it only during the day."

"People have begged me to ask you many things," Lucia said. "The cure of some sick persons, of a deaf-mute . . ."

"Some I will cure, others not. In October I shall perform a miracle so that everyone may believe."

The briefest of the six apparitions was over and Lucia rose saying: "If you wish to see her, look in that direction." Her finger pointed to the eastern sky. Everyone could see the same luminous globe gliding off into the distance. "We felt truly happy," said the Vicar General of Leiria. "My friend, full of enthusiasm, went from group to group . . . asking people what they had seen. The persons asked came from the most varied social classes and all unanimously affirmed the reality of the phenomena which we ourselves had observed."

During the following weeks the homes of the three children were continually besieged by crowds of people demanding to question them. Only infrequently were the children able to escape their endless interrogations; otherwise they would suffer the non-stop barrage of questions with all the patience they could muster and offer the sacrifice to God. When Lucia told Francisco that Our Lord was coming in October the little boy joyfully exclaimed: "Oh, how wonderful! We have only seen Him twice and I love Him so much! . . . But look, how sad He still is. I am so sorry to see Him sad. I offer Him all the sacrifices I can think of. Sometimes I don't even run away from these people so as to make sacrifices."

A certain lawyer, Dr. Carlos Mendes, has left us a charming description of the three children at this time. Writing to his fiancée he recalled how he had entered the Marto's home and met Jacinta and Lucia. "The little mite (i.e., Jacinta) didn't want to come without her cousin (they are inseparable), and her sister had to coax her along. Very tiny, very babyish and shy, she came up to me. I sat down so as to see her better . . . and observe her at will. I must tell you, she is a little angel, a darling . . . Many times I have thought it and sometimes said it, that if you were to see and speak to her, you'd steal her, if it were possible! . . . She had a red flowered handkerchief on her head, the points tied behind. It was rather torn and old, and her coat was not particularly clean. Her skirt was full and wide in the local manner . . . I wish I could describe her face to you, but I fear I cannot do so adequately . . . Her eyes are very dark and enchantingly vivacious, while her expression is really angelic, so extraordinary sweet and kind that one is attracted to her, without knowing why. She was so shy and timid . . . Lucia wasn't there, so she wasn't at ease . . .

"Francisco arrived. His head was well covered by a cap, he wore a very short jacket, the waistcoat open and showing his shirt and narrow trousers — in fact, a little man in miniature. He has a splendid boyish face and his expression is both lively and manly. He answered my questions with confidence, and then Jacinta, too, began to gain courage. Shortly afterwards, Lucia arrived. You cannot imagine Jacinta's joy when she saw her!. . . Lucia is not very impressive to look at. Her expression is lively, but for the rest she is ordinary looking, typical of the region. She, too, was shy to begin with, but I soon put her at her ease, and then they all responded without any embarrassment and satisfied my curiosity.

"The naturalness and simplicity with which they speak and tell all that they saw, is extraordinary and impressive. Lucia sees the Lady, speaks to her and hears her. Jacinta sees the Lady, hears her, but does not address her. Francisco sees the Lady, but neither hears nor speaks to her . . . To hear these children, to see their candour and to observe them in general, makes such a remarkable impression on us that we are led to conclude that there is indeed something supernatural in all that they say. To be with them is an intensely moving experience . . .

"We then went with the children to the place of the apparitions to pray the rosary . . . The little holm oak tree has been reduced to almost nothing. Some flower pots containing sweet basil and other blossoms stood on a little stone wall around it. The three children knelt down. Lucia, who was in the middle, began to pray the rosary. The recollection, the fervour with which she prayed, impressed us deeply. It was for the soldiers who were in the war. With what devotion the rosary was prayed there! I don't think I ever prayed with so much attention . . ."

Some visitors to Aljustrel were not so friendly or inquisitive. They were the agents of the anti-religious Government who lost no time intimidating or threatening the children and their parents with arrest and even death if they went near the Cova da Iria again. At one stage, Ti Marto and his wife thought of sending the children away, but Francisco and Jacinta seemed not in the least affected by such threats. "If they kill us," they would say, "we'll go to Heaven all the sooner."

On 27 September the children were visited by Canon Formigão who interrogated each of them in turn. He dealt with Francisco first.

"What did you see at the Cova da Iria these last months?"

"I saw Our Lady."

"Where does she appear?"

"On top of the holm oak."

"Does she appear suddenly, or do you see her coming from somewhere?"

"I see her coming from the side where the sun rises and place herself on the holm oak."

"Does she come slowly or quickly?"

"She always comes quickly."

"Do you hear what she says to Lucia?"

"No."

"Do you ever speak to the Lady? Does she ever speak to you?"

"No. I have never asked her anything: she speaks only to Lucia."

"At whom does she look? Also at you and at Jacinta, or only at Lucia?"

"She looks at all three of us, but longer at Lucia."

"Does she ever cry or smile?"

"Neither one or the other. She is always grave."

"How is she dressed?"

"She has a long dress and over it a veil which covers her head and falls to the edges of her dress."

"What is the colour of the dress and the veil?"

"White, and the dress has gold lines."

"What is her attitude?"

"Like someone praying. She has her hands at the height of her breast."

"Does she hold anything in her hands?"

"She carries a rosary round the palm and the back of her right hand. It hangs down over her dress."

"What colour is the rosary?"

"It is white."

"Is the Lady beautiful?"

"Yes, she is."

"More beautiful than that little girl over there?"

"More beautiful than anyone I have ever seen."

Jacinta was then brought in and she corroborated what her brother had said. The canon asked her what was the chief thing that the Lady had said and the child replied: "That we were to say the rosary every day." When it was Lucia's turn to be questioned, her answers again agreed with Francisco's, but she added a few extra details.

"How long does she stay?" the canon enquired. "A long time or short?"

"Short."

"Enough to say an Our Father and Hail Mary, or more?"

"A good deal more, but not always the same time. Perhaps it would not be long enough to say a rosary (five decades)."

"The first time you saw her, were you frightened?"

"I was, so much so that I wanted to run away with Jacinta and Francisco, but she said we must not be afraid because she would not hurt us. She wore a white dress coming down to her feet and her head is covered by a veil of the same colour and length."

. . . "Did she tell you or your cousins to say certain prayers?"

"She told us to say the rosary in honour of Our Lady of the Rosary to obtain peace for the world."

"Did she say that many people should be present during the apparitions in the Cova da Iria?"

"She said nothing about that."

"Is it true that she told you a secret that you were not to tell to anyone whomsoever?"

"That is true."

"Does it concern you or your cousins also?"

"All three."

. . . "Why do you often lower your eyes instead of keeping them on the Lady?"

"Because she sometimes blinds me."

"Did she teach you a prayer?"

"Yes. She wished us to say it after each decade of the rosary."

"Do you know it by heart?"

"Yes. O my Jesus, forgive us our sins, save us from the fires of Hell and lead all souls to Heaven, especially those most in need."

This and subsequent interviews by the Canon are too lengthy to be recorded here, but the above conveys a broad outline of a typical interrogation to which the children were subjected. The Canon was profoundly impressed and resolved to be present in the Cova da Iria on 13 October to see if the promised miracle materialised.

The entire country was now galvanised into preparation for the expected prodigy on 13 October. By the 12th, tens of thousands were converging on Fatima from all points of the compass despite appalling weather conditions. Driven by a fierce wind, sheets of rain lashed the countryside, turning the Cova into a vast quagmire. That morning, Lucia's mother, still tormented by an agony of disbelief in the apparitions, counselled her daughter to go to confession "because if there is no miracle, we will all be killed." The child's response was predictable. "I will go with you if you wish, but not because I am afraid. Our Lady will keep her word."

By the morning of 13 October an immense multitude had assembled in the Cova da Iria. They prayed and sang hymns as they huddled and shivered under their umbrellas in the furiously lashing rain. Thousands of latecomers struggled to gain vantage points around the muddied rim of the Cova. Meanwhile, the three children were carried shoulder-high in their sodden, mud-splattered clothes, through the seething mass of humanity amid tumultuous scenes. Everyone wanted to touch the little seers and cry out their petitions for Our Lady. The crush was so great that Jacinta began to weep. "Look after my father!" she kept crying, seeing Ti Marto hard pressed from behind. As they neared the holm oak, their progress became a nightmare of thrusting shoulders, grabbing hands, drenching rain, squelching mud and a deafening cacophony of imploring cries. The men bearing the children had to splash part of their way through pools of water up to two feet deep.

Finally they reached their destination and the children were put down in the thick mud and crush of elbowing bodies. Lucia began to recite the rosary, then suddenly cried out: "Put down your umbrellas everyone!" And to Jacinta and Francisco: "Kneel down. Our Lady is coming! I have seen the flash!" Lucia's mother, in an anguish of uncertainty, shrilled from behind: "Look closely, my child. Take care you make no mistake." But her daughter was already in ecstasy. A white mist developed around the children to a height of some fifteen feet and Lucia was heard to say: "What do you want of me?"

The Lady was shining before the three children in all her glowing splendour and while they beheld her sad, compassionate gaze, the vast multitude saw the numerous heavenly signs which attended each vision. "I am the Lady of the Rosary," she said. "I would like a chapel built here in my honour. Continue to pray the rosary every day." She added that the war would soon be ending and that the soldiers would not be long returning to their homes. Lucia began to mention the numerous petitions she had been given and the Lady answered that she would grant some, but what was so important was that "men must amend their lives and ask pardon for their sins." She then uttered a last imploring heart-cry which summed up the message and meaning of her appearances. "Do not offend God anymore, for He is already too greatly offended."

Having said this, she rose and turning, threw beams of light towards the sun. Instinctively, Lucia cried out in ecstasy: "Oh, look at the sun!" The multitude suddenly saw the black clouds tear apart like drawn curtains and the sun stand forth unchallenged for everyone to see. It did not dazzle the eye; one could look on it as on the moon. All at once, the mighty star of day began to tremble, to move to and fro across the sky, throwing out great shafts of multiple-coloured light in thousands of beautifully hued squares which flooded the sky, the drab landscape and the peoples' clothing. The sun was now whirling like a gigantic fire-wheel, furiously casting off the most magnificent beams of coloured light in all directions. After a few minutes, it suddenly stopped, then resumed its fantastic gyrations a second time, more brilliant and colourful than before. Again it paused, then as if taking on new life, it became a hurtling dynamo of incredible colours, falling everywhere like an exploding rainbow. The spellbound crowd watched this unbelievable spectacle for some twelve minutes.

All at once, the sun detached itself from the sky and came plunging zig-zaggedly down on the screaming multitude like a monstrous fireball. Everywhere people were falling into the mud in panic, crying out their sins and pleading for divine mercy as they cringed in imminent expectation of the end of the world. As we shall see in the next chapter, these were minutes of indescribable confusion and terror. At the last moment the sun arrested its death plunge and climbed back into the sky to resume its normal position and brightness. And as the crowd heaved a vast sigh of relief, everyone noticed that their clothes and the entire Cova da Iria were completely dry.

While all this was going on, the children beheld the mysteries of the rosary in tableaux form in the sky. First they saw the Holy Family to represent the Joyful mysteries, then Our Lord carrying His cross with Our Lady of Sorrows to represent the Sorrowful mysteries. Finally, Lucia alone was privileged to see Our Lady of Mount Carmel holding out the Brown Scapular to the world, to signify the Glorious mysteries. Since the spirit of Carmel signifies triumph over suffering, it may be that Lucia alone was privileged to see this vision because only she will live to see the promised triumph of the Immaculate Heart of Mary. This is conjecture of course, but it cannot be ruled out.

After the miracle was over, the children were besieged on all sides by demanding questions and hands clawing at their clothing for relics. In the middle of this commotion, Lucia was asked if the war would end that day and the poor child, almost at her wits end, blurted out unthinkingly "yes". This incident has been pounced upon by exacting critics as "a serious difficulty" to the Fatima story, whereas the truth is quite different. On 18 May 1941, Lucia wrote to her superior explaining that she had "lost the thread a little" of what Our Lady was saying and almost interrupted her at one stage. Jacinta afterwards reminded her of what Our Lady had really said, viz. "The war will end *soon*." (See *Memoirs and Letters of Sister Lucia,* Professor A. Martins S.J., 1973, page 443, and *Fatima 1917-68: Histoire complete des apparitions et de leurs suites,* Toulouse, pp. 138-141, by Canon Bathas.)

V

THE SOLAR MIRACLE

THE miracle of the sun on 13 October 1917 was the great heavenly sign given by God to confirm the reality of the Divine intervention at Fatima and the seriousness of His message for mankind. Since the implications of the stupendous phenomenon are so profound and far-reaching, it is imperative that we examine it in some detail.

The preliminary manifestations seen in the earlier apparitions were impressive enough: the multitude of colours flooding the sky and landscape, the luminous flashes and roars of thunder, the bending of the shrub (13 June), the celestial fragrance (19 August), the luminous globe and rain of vanishing roses (13 September) and the abating of the sunlight and cooling of the air (in all the apparitions). But now, to climax everything, there occurred a firmament-cracking spectacle of unprecedented magnitude.

Three times, as we have seen, Our Lady had promised to perform a miracle so that "everyone may believe" in the reality of her appearances. The children duly announced the news, which spread through Portugal like a prairie fire and flared across the pages of the anti-clerical press. As far as is known, *for the very first time in recorded history, a prophet or seer was asking all the people to assemble at a certain place and time to witness a public miracle to prove that the message which had been received came from God.* The prediction created intense controversy everywhere. The revolutionary Government, which had vowed to stamp out religion in two generations, were taking no chances with what they regarded as sheer religious fanaticism. Armed soldiers were sent to the Cova da Iria on the morning of 13 October to prevent people gathering there. The press lampooned the whole affair and loudly predicted that a non-occurring miracle would finally explode the myth of religion.

But word of the extraordinary happenings in the Cova da Iria on the 13th of previous months had gripped the attention of vast numbers of believers. Tens of thousands converged on Fatima on the morning of 13 October, despite appalling weather conditions and the armed guards at the Cova da Iria. The latter were eventually swamped by a tidal wave of humanity. Fortunately for posterity, reporters of the anti-clerical press turned up in force, fully expecting to record a colossal fiasco.

The word miracle as used by the Mother of God, must be understood in its absolute sense — an extraordinary event either above, contrary to, or outside nature. "Those effects are rightly to be termed miracles," says St. Thomas Aquinas, "which are wrought by divine power apart from the order usually observed in nature." (*Contra Gent.*, III. cii). In the case of the solar miracle of 13 October 1917, we have seen how a ball of fire resembling the sun whirled in the sky amid a multitude of wavering colours which flooded the sky and landscape, as if the scene was being viewed through the stained glass windows of some beautiful cathedral. At the climax the fire fell earthwards, causing the screaming multitude to hurl themselves into the mud in imminent expectation of the end of the world.

This was only the third time in history that God had used the sun to perform a miracle — the other two occasions being the prolongation of daylight at the prayer of Joshua (Joshua 10), and the sign given to the King of Judah in 714 B.C. by the prophet Ezekiel in which the shadow of a sundial retraced its path by ten hours. (Kings 4:20). But what made the Fatima miracle unique was that its exact time and location were publicly announced months in advance.

To gain an accurate appreciation of all that happened that day, it is necessary to rely on the testimonies of those who were present — believers and agnostics. Because of the exceptional importance of this evidence, it is recounted in some detail to give the reader a glimpse of the same spectacle from varying angles. The cumulative evidence cited here should help to bring home to us not only the searing actuality of this event, but the crucial importance of the message that the miracle was meant to project.

We will begin by quoting two rather lengthy reports carried by the leading anti-clerical newspapers of the time, since they convey a graphic description of the scene on that memorable day. The first is from the *Diario de Noticias (Daily News)* of 15 October 1917. This newspaper commanded the largest circulation in Portugal at the time. The headline read: "The 'Miracle' of Fatima. More than fifty thousand people gather at the place of the apparitions."[1]

"Vila Nova de Ourém, 13 October. In spite of the fitful, drizzling rain that began to fall early in the morning, an extraordinary gathering of people assembled in the parish of Fatima to witness the unusual happening of an apparition that ever since Ascension Thursday had claimed the attention of the people and attracted thousands of pilgrims of all classes of society, age and sex, to the locality. The day before yesterday, groups of people began to pass through this little town, men and women who went their way singing hymns and praying the rosary with great faith and devotion, in the direction of the place where the 'miracle' which, according to the declarations of the three little shepherds to whom Our Lady deigned to appear several times as they say, on each 13th of the month, would occur. The air of expectancy was evident as the noontime encounter approached. Although the rain continued to pour down, not one of all that multitude moved a step from that favoured spot. Precisely at that same moment, the three little shepherds, whose names are Lucia, Jacinta and Francisco, arrived at the exact spot, falling immediately to their knees beneath an arch erected for the occasion, with an altar close by.

"A wave of emotion seemed to take hold of those many thousands of believers and curious alike. As a great number of people had their umbrellas open, the little ones asked the people to shut them. Then an extraordinary thing happened. According to the testimony of thousands and thousands present there, the sun appeared like a dull silver plate spinning round in a circular movement as if it were moved by electricity, according to the expression used by knowledgeable people who witnessed the fact.

"Then thousands of people, swayed by emotion and who knows, even dazzled by the light of the sun that had appeared for the first time that day, fell to the ground, weeping and raising their hands, joined instinctively in prayer. On their faces an expression of ecstatic rapture could be observed, denoting absolute alienation from life. Their simple hearts prayed and wept in the presence of this strange sensation of a fact that for them, at the moment, was miraculous. According to what we heard, there were people who seemed to see the sun leave its supposed orbit, break through the clouds and descend to the horizon. The impression of these seers spread to others, in a common effort to explain the phenomenon, many crying out in fear that the giant orb would precipitate itself to the earth on top of them, and imploring the protection of the Holy Virgin. The 'miraculous hour' passed.

"Then the children rose up smiling, and explained to their anxious listeners that the Lady had said that peace would come soon and it would not be long before our brave soldiers would return from France where they were fighting so courageously . . . After these moments of anxiety, the pilgrims returned to their homes, longing to tell those who hadn't the good forture to journey to the holy place, of what their eyes and above all their believing souls had so astoundingly witnessed."

While the writer of this account was careful not to involve himself personally in the recognition of the miracle lest he compromise himself before his anti-religious superiors in Lisbon, the editor of another Government newspaper *O Seculo (The Century)* was not so restrained. On 15 October the headline on the front page read: "Terrifying Event! How the sun danced at midday in the sky of Fatima." The account continued:

"Along the road from the Chao de Macas station, we met the first groups going to the holy place, a distance of more than ten miles. Men and women walked along barefoot, with the women carrying their bags on their heads, topped with their heavy shoes, while the men leaned on their sturdy staffs and carried umbrellas as a precaution. They seemed unaware of all that happened around them, disinterested in either the landscape or the other wayfarers, saying the rosary in a sad rhythm, as if immersed in a dream . . . With slow, cadenced steps, they threaded their way along the dusty road, among pine groves and olive orchards, so that they might arrive before nightfall at the place of the apparition. There, in the open, under the cold light of the stars, they planned to sleep and get the best places next day near the blessed holm oak, and thus have a better view.

"As they entered the town of Vila Nova de Ourém, some women, already infected with the germ of atheism, joked about the great event. 'Aren't you going tomorrow to see the saint?' one asked. 'Me? No! Not unless she comes to see me!' They laughed heartily, while the devout passed on, indifferent to anything that was not the motive of their pilgrimage.

"Only by a sheer stroke of luck or kindness could lodging be found in Ourém. All night long, the most varied type of vehicles moved into the town square, carrying the faithful and the curious, besides the old ladies somberly dressed, weighed down by the years, but with the ardent fire of faith shining in their eyes, which gave them heart to leave for a day the little corner in the home from which they were inseparable.

"At dawn, new groups surged, undaunted, and crossed through the village without stopping for a moment, breaking the early morning silence with their beautiful hymns, the delicate harmony of the women's voices making a violent contrast with their rustic appearance. The sun was rising, though the skies presaged a storm. Dark clouds loomed directly over Fatima. Nothing would stop the crowd converging from every direction on towards the holy place, utilising every means of transport. Luxurious automobiles glided swiftly along the road, their horns sounding continually, while oxcarts dragged slowly alongside them. There were carriages of all types, victoria chaises, landaus, and wagons fitted out with seats for the occasion and crowded to the limit . . . Donkeys trotted along the side of the road, and the countless cyclists performed real feats to keep from colliding with the vehicles.

"By ten o'clock the sky was completely hidden behind the clouds, and the rain began to fall in earnest. Swept by a strong wind and beating upon the faces of the people, it soaked the roadway and the pilgrims to the marrow of their bones . . . But no one complained or turned back, and if some took shelter under trees or walls, the great majority continued on their journey with remarkable indifference to the rain . . . The place where the Virgin was alleged to have appeared is fronted to a large extent by the road which leads to Leiria, along which the vehicles bringing the pilgrims were parked. More than a hundred cars could be counted, more than a hundred bicycles, and countless numbers of other types of conveyance, among which was a bus from Torres Novas bringing a group of people of every social condition. But the great mass of the people coming from great distances, the Minho and Beira in the north, Alentejo and Algarve in the south, congregated round the holm oak tree, which, according to the children, was the pedestal chosen by the Virgin. It could be considered the centre of a large circle round which the spectators gathered to watch events.

"Seen from the road, the general effect was picturesque. The peasants sheltering under their huge umbrellas, accompanied the unloading of their provisions with the singing of hymns and the recitation of the decades of the rosary in a matter-of-fact way. People plodded through the sticky clay in order to see the famous holm oak with its wooden arch and hanging lanterns, at closer quarters . . . Where were the little shepherds? Lucia, 10 years old, and her little companions, Francisco, aged 9, and Jacinta, aged 7, had not yet arrived. Finally, about half an hour before the time when the apparition would take place, their presence was noted. The girls wore wreaths of flowers and looked like angels as they moved towards the arch. The rain fell unceasingly, but nobody minded.

"Latecomers were still arriving in cars. Groups of people were kneeling in the mud, quite unconcerned. Moved by an interior guidance, Lucia asked the people to shut their umbrellas, and in spite of the rain, she was promptly obeyed. There were so many people there, praying in such earnestness, almost in ecstasy as if their dry lips could no longer move, their hands joined, their eyes wide with wonder, people who seemed to be overpowered by the supernatural. The child asserted that the Lady had spoken to her once more, and then the sky, still overcast, began to clear overhead. The rain ceased, and the sunlight illuminated the whole landscape with all the sombre effects of a wintry morning . . .

"From the road where the vehicles were parked and where hundreds of people who had not dared to brave the mud were congregated, one could see the immense throng turn towards the sun, which appeared free from clouds and in its zenith. It looked like a plaque of dull silver, and it was possible to look at it without the least discomfort. It neither burned nor blinded the eyes . . . At

that moment, a great shout went up and one could hear the spectators nearest at hand shouting: 'A miracle! A miracle!'

"Before the astonished eyes of the crowd, whose aspect was
biblical as they stood bareheaded, pale with fright, eagerly searching the sky, the sun trembled, made sudden incredible movements
outside all cosmic laws — the sun 'danced' according to the typical
expression of the people. Standing at the step of the Torres Novas
bus was an old man, whose appearance in face and figure
reminded one of Paul Deroulede. With his face turned towards the
sun he recited the Creed in a loud voice . . . Afterwards, I saw
him going up to those around him who still had their hats on, and
vehemently imploring them to uncover their heads before such an
extraordinary demonstration of the existence of God. Identical
scenes were repeated elsewhere, and in one place, a woman cried
out in a gasp of surprise: 'How dreadful that there are some men
who do not even bare their heads before such a stupendous
miracle!' People then began to ask each other what they had seen.
The great majority admitted to having seen the trembling and the
dancing of the sun. Others affirmed that they saw the face of the
Blessed Virgin, while others swore that the sun whirled on itself
like a giant catherine wheel and that it lowered itself to the earth
as if to burn it with its rays. Some said they saw it change colours
successively.

"It was almost three o'clock in the afternoon. The sky was swept
clear of clouds and the sun followed its course in its usual
splendour, so that no one ventured to gaze at it directly. What
about the little shepherds? Lucia, who had spoken to Our Lady,
was announcing with expressive gestures, as she was carried along
shoulder-high by a man and passed from group to group, that the
war would end and that the soldiers would return . . . But news
like that, however, did nothing to increase the jubilation of those
who heard it. The heavenly sign was sufficient for them: it was
everything.

"Intense curiosity prevailed to see the two little girls in their
wreaths of roses, and to kiss the hands of these 'little saints', one of
whom, Jacinta, seemed nearer to fainting than dancing. They had
so longed to see the sign from Heaven: they had seen and were
satisfied and radiated their burning faith . . . The crowd dis-
persed rapidly, without any difficulty, without any sign of dis-
order, without any need for policemen to regulate them. Those
who were the first to arrive were also the first to depart, running
out on the roadway, travelling on foot with their footwear in a
bundle on their heads or strung from their staffs. They went, with
hearts overflowing with joy, to bring the good news to their
hamlets that had not been wholly depopulated for the time being.

"And what of the priests? Some turned up at the place, ming-

ling more among the curious spectators rather than among the
pilgrims avid for heavenly signs and favours. Perhaps neither one
nor the other succeeded in concealing their happiness, which so
often transpired in triumphant guise . . . It only remains for those
competent to do justice to the bewildering dance of the sun which,
on this day in Fatima, caused Hosannas to resound from the hearts
of all the faithful present, and naturally made a great impression,
as people worthy of belief assured me, on the freethinkers and
others without any religious conviction who had come to this now
famous spot located on the poor pastureland high up on the serra.

Avelino de Almeida."

This report created a considerable reaction among the atheist
authorities in Lisbon and Sr. Almeida was bitterly attacked for
daring to admit that there had been a supernatural manifestation.
But his impartiality had been demonstrated by the fact that on the
morning of the miracle, he had published an article on the front
page of *O Seculo* in which he had quietly dismissed the reported
visions and the possibility of a miracle. Later, at the request of a
friend, he wrote another account of what happened that day which
was published in the *Illustração Portuguesa* of 29 October 1917.

"You write and ask me to tell you, sincerely and minutely, what
I saw and heard in the barren pastureland of Fatima, when the
fame of the heavenly apparitions had congregated in that desolate
wilderness tens of thousands of people . . . Members of your
family dragged you with them to Fatima among that immense
ocean of people who gathered there on 13 October. Your reason-
ing suffered a formidable blow, and you want to form a secure
opinion, enlisting the aid of unbiased evidence such as mine. For I
was there only in the discharge of a very difficult mission: that of
relating impartially for the notable daily paper *O Seculo,* the facts
that occurred before me, and all the surrounding unusual and
elucidating details connected with them . . . What was it that I
heard and that brought me to Fatima? I heard that the Virgin Mary
had appeared after the feast of the Ascension to three little shepherds who were pasturing their flock, two little girls and a lad. She
recommended them to pray, and promised to appear there on the
holm oak on the 13th day of each month until October, when she
would give them some sign of the power of God and would make
revelations. This news was spread all round for many miles, then
flew like wildfire from place to place throughout Portugal. The
number of believers increased month by month, coming on pilgrimage to this poor barren spot, so that by 13 October, about
50,000 people at least had gathered there, according to the
calculations of some impartial individuals . . .

"I saw the multitude, densely massed around the little miraculous holm oak and plucking its branches to keep as relics, or overflowing through the immense pastureland, traversed and dominated by the road from Leiria, and which now presented the most picturesque and varied concourse of cars and people that thronged it on that never-to-be-forgotten day, all awaiting in orderly fashion the supernatural manifestations, without fearing that the wintry weather would do any harm or diminish their splendour or magnificence . . . At the hour foretold, the rain ceased to fall, the dense mass of clouds parted, and the sun — like a shining disc of dull silver — appeared at its full zenith, and began to whirl around in a wild and violent dance, that a large number of people likened to a carnival display, with such lovely glowing colours passing successively over the sun's surface. A miracle, as the crowd cried out; or a natural phenomenon, as the learned say? It is not important for me to know the answer now, but only to tell you and confirm what I saw . . . The rest we leave to science and the Church."

That many intellectuals postulated a natural explanation for the solar phenomenon was due to their refusal to recognise the possibility of a supernatural origin. One of them, Professor Frederico Oom of the faculty of sciences and director of the Lisbon Observatory stated in *O Seculo* shortly afterwards: "If it were a cosmic phenomenon, astronomical and meteorological observatories would not have failed to record it. And this is precisely what is missing: that inevitable recording of all the disturbances in the world system, no matter how small they may be . . .". The scientist added that the phenomenon might have been of a psychological nature "but is completely foreign to the branch of science that I cultivate." However, the theory of auto-suggestion which other intellectuals also advanced, was found to be wanting when it was discovered that the miracle had been seen over a 600 square mile area by people not at all interested in the happenings at Fatima. And there were impartial intellectuals in the Cova da Iria that day who were honest enough to admit the reality of the miracle. Among them was Dr. Joseph Garrett, Professor of Natural Sciences at Coimbra University, who wrote the following account in December 1917:

"I am going to relate to you in a brief and concise manner, without any statements which would conceal the truth, what I saw in Fatima on 13 October 1917 . . . I arrived at midday. The rain which had fallen persistently all morning, combined with a blustery wind, continued fretfully, as if threatening to drown everyone. The dull and heavy sky, its dark-grey clouds water-laden, predicted abundant rain for a long time to come.

"I remained on the road in the shelter of the hood of my car, looking rather disdainfully towards the place where they said the apparition would be seen, not daring to step on to the sodden and muddy earth of the freshly-ploughed field. I was a little more than a hundred metres from the high wooden posts mounted by a rough cross, seeing distinctly the wide circle of people who, with their umbrellas open, seemed like a vast arena of mushrooms. A little after one o'clock,[2] the children to whom Our Lady, as they declare, appeared and appointed the place, day and hour of the apparition, arrived at the site. Hymns were intoned and sung by the people who gathered about them. At a certain moment, this immense mass of people, so varied and compact, closed their umbrellas and uncovered their heads in a gesture that could have been one of humility or respect, but which left me surprised and bewildered, because now the rain, with a blind persistency, poured down on their heads and drenched them through.

"Later, I was told that this crowd, who finished up by kneeling in the mud, had obeyed the voice of a child. It must have been about half past one when there rose up, on the precise spot where the children were, a pillar of smoke, a delicate, slender, bluish column that went straight up to about two metres, perhaps above their heads and then evaporated. The phenomenon lasted for some seconds and was perfectly visible to the naked eye . . . It was repeated yet a second and third time. On these three occasions, and especially on the last one, the slender posts stood out distinctly in the dull grey atmosphere.

"While I continued looking at the place of the apparitions in a serene, if cold expectation of something happening, and with diminishing curiosity, because a long time had passed without anything to excite my attention, I heard a shout from thousands of voices, and saw the multitude which straggled out at my feet, here and there concentrated in small groups round the trees, suddenly turn its back on the point towards which, up to now, it had directed its attention, and turn to look at the sky on the opposite side . . . The sun, a few moments before, had broken through the thick layer of clouds that hid it and shone clearly and intensely. I veered towards the magnet which seemed to be drawing all eyes, and saw it as a disc with clear-cut rim, luminous and shining, but which did not hurt the eyes . . .

"It looked like a glazed circular piece cut from a mother-of-pearl shell . . . It could not be confused either, with the sun seen through fog (for there was no fog at the time), because it was not opaque, diffused or veiled . . . The sky was mottled with light cirrus clouds, the blue coming through here and there, but sometimes the sun stood out in patches of clear sky . . . It was a remarkable fact that one could fix one's eyes on this brazier of heat and light without any pain in the eyes or blinding of the retina

. . . The sun's disc did not remain immobile. This was not the sparkling of a heavenly body, for it spun round on itself in a mad whirl, when suddenly a clamour was heard from all the people. The sun, whirling, seemed to loosen itself from the firmament and advance threateningly upon the earth as if to crush us with its huge fiery weight. The sensation during these moments was terrible.

"During the solar phenomenon, which I have just described in detail, there were changes of colour in the atmosphere . . . Looking at the sun, I noticed that everything around was becoming darkened. I looked first at the nearest objects and then extended my glance further afield as far as the horizon. I saw everything an amethyst colour. Objects around me, the sky and the atmosphere, were of the same colour. An oak tree nearby threw a shadow of this colour on the ground. Fearing that I was suffering from an affection of the retina . . . I turned away and shut my eyes, keeping my hands over them to intercept the light. With my back still turned, I opened my eyes and saw that the landscape was the same purple colour as before . . . Soon after, I heard a peasant who was near me shout out in tones of astonishment: 'Look, that lady is all yellow!' In fact, everything both near and far, had changed, taking on the colour of old yellow damask. People looked as if they were suffering from jaundice, and I recall my amusement at seeing them look so ugly and unattractive. Laughter was heard. My own hand was of the same yellow colour . . .

"All these phenomena which I have described, were observed by me in a calm and serene state of mind and without any emotional disturbance. It is for others to interpret and explain them."

Let us look briefly at two more newspaper reports before we hear the testimony of the believers present. The *Ordem* stated:

"The sun, at one moment surrounded by scarlet flames, at another, aureoled in yellow and deep purple, seemed to be moving very fast and spinning: at times it seemed to be loosed from the sky and to approach the earth, radiating a great heat."

The Lisbon paper *O Dia* wrote:

"At midday by the sun, the rain stopped. The sky, pearly grey in colour, illuminated the vast arid landscape with a strange light. The sun had a transparent gauzy veil so that the eye could easily be fixed on it. The grey mother-of-pearl tone turned into a sheet of silver which broke up as the clouds were parted and the silver sun, enveloped in the same gauzy grey light, was seen to whirl and turn in the circle of broken clouds. A cry went up from every mouth and people fell on their knees on the muddy ground . . . The light turned a beautiful blue as though through the window of a cathedral. The blue faded slowly and then the light seemed to pass through yellow glass. Yellow stain fell on white handkerchiefs against the dark skirts of the women. The colours were repeated on the stones and on the serra."

Another eyewitness who was not at all disposed to expecting a miracle, the Baron of Alvaiazere, carefully took all the precautions spelt out by Gustave le Bon in his *Psychology of the Crowd.* He stated in a deposition to the canonical committee investigating the apparitions: ". . . An indescribable impression overtook me. I only know that I cried out: I believe! I believe! And tears ran from my eyes. I was amazed, in ecstasy before the demonstration of Divine power . . . converted in that moment."

Present in the Cova da Iria that morning was Dr. Formigão, Professor of the seminary at Santarem, who had earlier questioned the three children.

"As if like a bolt from the blue," he wrote, "the clouds were wrenched apart, and the sun at its zenith appeared in all its splendour. It began to revolve vertiginously on its axis, like the most magnificent firewheel that could be imagined, taking on all the colours of the rainbow and sending forth multi-coloured flashes of light, producing the most astounding effect. This sublime and incomparable spectacle, which was repeated three distinct times, lasted for about ten minutes. The immense multitude, overcome by the evidence of such a tremendous prodigy, threw themselves on their knees. The Creed, the Hail Mary, acts of contrition, burst from all lips, and tears, tears of thanksgiving and repentance sprang from all eyes."

Another prominent witness was John Carreira, whose mother had asked Lucia in June 1917 to petition Our Lady to cure him of his lameness or give him a livelihood. (The latter plea was answered and he became the sacristan of the shrine for nearly fifty years). On 13 October 1917, John found himself pressed against the three children by the crowd "with my knees jammed between Lucia's and Francisco's feet." He added: "I saw the sun spinning round and it seemed about to come down on us. It revolved like a bicycle wheel. Afterwards, it returned to its place . . . I wasn't afraid, but I heard people cry out: 'Oh, we are going to die! We are going to die!'"

John Haffert, International Lay Delegate of the Blue Army of Our Lady of Fatima, gathered the testimony of many eyewitnesses of the miracle into an extraordinary book which he wrote in 1960.[3] These accounts give an even more graphic picture of that fearful moment, with people crying out their sins and imploring pardon, as if at the point of death. We record a few of them as follows:

"I saw the sun as if it were a ball of fire, begin to move in the clouds. It had been raining all morning and the sky was full of clouds, but the rain had stopped. It lasted for several seconds, crushingly pressing down on us. Wan faces, standing here, from every side great ejaculations, acts of contrition, of the love of God. An indescribable moment! We feel it. We remain dominated by it. But it is not possible to describe it."

Carlos Mendes, lawyer.

"I looked at the sun and saw it spinning like a disc, rolling on itself. I saw people changing colour. They were stained with the colours of the rainbow. The sun seemed to fall down from the sky . . . The people said that the world was going to end . . . They were afraid and screaming."

Antonio de Oliveiro, farmer.

"I saw the sun turn upon itself; it seemed to fall from the sky . . . The people around me were crying that the world was going to end."

Maria dos Prazeres, widow.

"The sun started to roll from one place to another and changed to blue, yellow — all colours. Then we see the sun coming towards the children. Everyone was crying out. Some started to confess their sins because there was no priest around there . . . My mother grabbed me to her and started to cry, saying: 'It is the end of the world!' And then we see the sun come right into the trees . . ."

Dominic Reis, in an American TV interview, 1960.[4]

"Suddenly the rain stopped and a great splendour appeared and the children cried: 'Look at the sun!' I saw the sun coming down, feeling that it was falling to the ground. At that moment, I collapsed."

Maria Candida da Silva.

"I looked and saw that the people were in various colours — yellow, white, blue. At the same time, I beheld the sun spinning at great speed and very near me. I at once thought: I am going to die."

Rev. Joao Menitra.

As we have noted earlier, the miracle was seen over a 600 square mile area, thus obviating the suggested explanation of collective hallucination. In the town of Leiria, eighteen miles away to the north-west, the miracle was seen as a great red flash due to the restricting contours of the land. Rev. Joaquim Lourenco, a canon lawyer of the diocese of Leiria in 1960, witnessed the miracle in the village of Alburitel, some nine miles distant. He was a school-boy at the time, and in 1960 he told John Haffert:

"I feel incapable of describing what I saw. I looked fixedly at the sun, which seemed pale and did not hurt my eyes. Looking like a ball of snow, revolving on itself, it suddenly seemed to come down in a zig-zag, menacing the earth. Terrified, I ran and hid myself among the people, who were weeping and expecting the end of the world at any moment. It was a crowd which had gathered outside our local village school, and we had all left classes and run into the streets because of the cries and surprised shouts of men and women who were in the street in front of the school when the miracle began.

"There was an unbeliever there who had spent the morning mocking the 'simpletons' who had gone off to Fatima just to see an ordinary girl. He now seemed paralysed, his eyes fixed on the sun. He began to tremble from head to foot, and lifting up his arms, fell on his knees in the mud, crying out to God. But meanwhile the people continued to cry out and to weep, asking God to pardon their sins. We all ran to the two chapels in the village, which were soon filled to overflowing. During those long moments of the solar prodigy, objects around us turned all colours of the rainbow . . ."

An American building contractor, Abano Barros, related to John Haffert in 1960 how he saw the miracle in a village near Minde, about eight miles from Fatima. "I was watching sheep, as was my daily task, and suddenly, there in the direction of Fatima, I saw the sun fall from the sky. I thought it was the end of the world."

At least one eyewitness, the poet Alfonso Lopes Viera, saw the miracle from a distance of 30 miles — at the ocean town of San Pedro der Muel. The author has also discovered at first hand that the miracle was seen in Pombal, some 32 miles to the north. Investigations have proved that it was visible over an area of approximately 32 miles by 20. The fact that it was not recorded beyond that distance, nor in any of the world's observatories, further confirms its extra-natural nature. Whether it actually was a miraculous transformation of the sun over a restricted area, or a divine representation of the sun that was seen, is unimportant since "nothing is impossible with God." (Luke 1:37). We do know however that not everyone present saw exactly the same thing. "I presume that each received what he or she was prepared for or what God knew to be needed," wrote Fr. Martindale, S.J.,[5] "as, maybe, when the Divine Voice spoke to Our Lord, some said: 'An angel spoke to Him, others that it thundered.' (John 12:29)."

Over the past half century, several scientific suggestions have been advanced in an attempt to explain the miracle, but none of them carry any weight. In the 1940s an Italian Jesuit scientist, Pio Sciatizzi, undertook an exhaustive study of the phenomenon and published his results in a book entitled *Fatima in the Light of Faith and Science.* Fr. Sciatizzi was a professor of algebra and trigonometry at the Gregorian University, Rome, and an outstanding mathematician and astronomer, highly esteemed in the Italian scientific world. He concluded:

"Of the historic reality of this event there can be no doubt whatsoever. That it was outside and against known laws can be proved by certain simple scientific considerations . . . Given the indubitable reference to God and the general context of the event, it seems that we must attribute to Him alone the most obvious and colossal miracle of history."

As we end this chapter, a sobering thought arises. Had the message and miracle occured at the time of Noah, the world might conceivably have been saved from the deluge. Now that it has happened when the mounting sins of humanity threaten the world with a nuclear deluge, we can, perhaps, better understand the insistent words of Pope Pius XII, underlining the intercessory power of Our Lady with God: "The compassionate and maternal Heart of Mary performed the miracle of Fatima."

NOTES

1. Dr. Garrett, whose testimony follows, scientifically estimated the crowd at 100,000.
2. There was a difference of about one and a half hours between sun time and legal Portuguese time.
3. *Meet the Witnesses,* by John Haffert, A.M.I. Press, Washington, N.J., U.S.A., 1961.
4. The author is in possession of a 16 mm sound film recording of this interview.
5. cf. *The Message of Fatima,* C. C. Martindale, S.J., Burns and Oates Ltd, London, 1950.

VI

FACING REALITY

IT IS now necessary to consider the significance of the solar miracle and the message it was meant to underscore in the light of the present crises convulsing the world and the Church. And perhaps the most dominant fact to strike the objective reader must surely be the sheer magnitude of Our Lady's intervention and its exact coincidence with the rise to power of Communism in Russia. While Lenin was seizing power in Moscow, the Mother of God was uttering those key words: "If my requests are heeded, Russia will be converted and there will be peace. Otherwise, Russia will spread her errors throughout the world, fomenting wars, revolutions and persecutions against the Church. The good will be martyred, the Holy Father will have much to suffer and various nations will be annihilated."

Sixty years later, only the final dread phrase of the prophecy remains unfulfilled. It may be averted altogether since the prophecy is conditional. But one cannot overlook the unprecedented wickedness of today's world and the deadly nuclear 'terror-go-round' which is its fateful consequence. Nor can we be accused of unjustified pessimism in spelling out the grim facts of the present world situation since popes, cardinals, statesmen, diplomats and seasoned news commentators have repeatedly warned of the possibility, even likelihood, of a global catastrophe in which entire nations would be annihilated. Yet despite this appalling prospect, the salvific message of Fatima, with its apocalyptic miracle of the sun and dazzling light of hope has, in many areas of the Church, scarcely evoked more than a flurry of sparks from the dull embers of mass apathy.

As far back as 1945, Pope Pius XII stated in a Christmas message to his cardinals: "The world is on the verge of a frightful abyss . . . Men must prepare themselves for suffering such as mankind has never seen." In speaking thus, the Holy Father (who was called "the Pope of Fatima") was fully aware of Our Lady's endorsement of the biblical lesson that war is a punishment for sin and that if the modern rebellion against God continued, Divine Justice would be compelled to punish mankind, even to the annihilation of entire nations.

On 25 September 1961, President Kennedy told the United Nations in New York: "Each one of the inhabitants of our planet should think now on the day when this world of ours will no longer be habitable. Every man, woman and child lives under the threat of a nuclear sword of Damocles, suspended by the most slender of threads, that could be cut at any moment by mere accident, by an error or miscalculation, or by sheer madness." These grim words were echoed in 1962 by the renowned nuclear physicist Bernard Philberth, in his book *Christian Prophecy and Nuclear Energy,* which went through many editions. "With nuclear energy," he wrote at the end of the book, "a possible end to our immediate surroundings looms up in an alarming manner." Another worthy authority, Eugene Ionesco, said at the opening of the 1972 Salzburg Festival (which the Austrian press hailed as "the most awaited speech"): "Hell is predominating today. Everything has become problematic. Any catastrophe is possible tomorrow. We live under the threat of cosmic destruction."

Side by side with this terrible threat is the danger of world Communism. In 1946 Sister Lucia herself told Dr. William Walsh, the eminent American historian, that unless the Fatima message was complied with by a sufficient number "every nation in the world without exception will eventually be enslaved and scourged by Communism." Successive statesmen have repeatedly warned of the growing threat of a pre-emptive nuclear attack by Russia which would defeat the West in less than twenty-four hours. Speaking from first hand experience of Communism, Cardinal Yu Pin, exiled Archbishop of Nanking, and Primate of all the Bishops of China, warned in 1978:

"A perspective of the world today does not exempt the United States from future control by Communism. The world is at the turning point of history and the fate of mankind hangs in the balance. Compromise with communist countries and providing help and moral support serves only one basic reality: greater strength for eventual world communist enslavement. We are in the last period of time sufficient to change the course of history and inspire a cry to *'wake up!'* Communism finds in religion today invaluable allies in its quest for global domination. The fantastic plan to turn the Church into an instrument of communist conquest would be unbelievable if we did not see it happening before our eyes. To have Catholics favourable to Marxism lends support to the Marxist cause on religious grounds. Some even present an image of Jesus as the 'subversive man from Nazareth' and are involved in organisations to help bring Marxism to power . . ."

His Eminence continued: "Pope Pius XI's penetrating and revealing analysis of Communism, exposing its evils and disregard for humanity, still remains today one of our most valuable documents on the truth of this diabolical system . . . Unfortunately, the warnings of Our Lady of Fatima and the teaching of Pope Pius XI have not been sufficiently appreciated. As a result, the infiltration and forces of Communism have been stronger and more terrible than at any other time. Communism has already spread through the entire world . . . We must encourage the faithful to pray fervently and promote the message of Fatima which the Blessed Virgin gave to the world in 1917, the same year that Russia as a government began, as predicted, to spread the errors of Communism throughout the world . . . The power of the Fatima message can convert the communist world . . . But perhaps before the end of the communist evil in the world, other nations and even the entire world may fall under its tyranny. Catholics must be prepared to suffer martyrdom."[1]

How grievous and enormous then must be the sins of our God-defying century for the warning of nuclear war and/or world Communism to be wrung from a God of love and mercy. How unspeakable must be the crimes and abominations of our age for the Omnipotent to hurl the sun terrifyingly towards earth, as if warning mankind in the most forceful manner conceivable of what would happen if the global storm of sin raged unabated and if Our Lady's pleas for prayer, penitence and reparation were brushed aside. Is this not the story of Sodom and Gomorrah all over again, with the Mother of God herself pleading for the ten just men to stand up and save the city of the world? Not long after that earth-shaking miracle, Pope Pius XI warned that "these are the worst days in the history of humanity since the deluge." And Pope John XXIII pleaded on 18 February 1959: "We exhort you to listen with simplicity of heart to the salutary warnings of the Mother of God".

Pope Paul VI believed that the fall of the sun at Fatima was not only a warning of possible nuclear war if mankind refused to change. "It was eschatological in the sense that it was like a repetition or an annunciation of a scene at the end of time for all humanity assembled together," His Holiness told the French philospher, Jean Guitton, on 28 May 1967, a statement which he later recorded in his book *Journal de ma Vie*. Those who would take exception to the Holy Father's words are obliged to ask themselves what greater sign would satisfy them. What could be more overwhelming in impact than the sun plunging like fire from Heaven while tens of thousands lay writhing in the mud, screaming for mercy, convinced that the end of the world had arrived? When an accident occurs, we try to understand what has happened, and why, through the evidence of eyewitnesses. At Fatima, we have 100,000 eyewitnesses of all faiths and none, united in their conviction that this was indeed the end of the world. And afterwards, when they found themselves alive and safe, but quivering with fear, they were seized by the realisation that God had stamped His Mother's words with a colossal preview of His second coming. Why then should we not ponder their unanimous testimony and take seriously to heart the crucial message which the solar miracle so heavily underscored? "While the death of God is proclaimed with arrogant glee," declared the Cardinal Patriarch of Lisbon at the 8th Fatima Congress at Kevelaer, Germany, on 18 September 1977, "Fatima appears like a great supernatural light. It is God who reveals Himself with the impressive majesty of Sinai."

Many authoritative commentators believe that the events of Fatima were a fulfillment of the twelfth chapter of the Apocalypse in which "a great sign appeared in Heaven, a woman clothed with the sun, with the moon under her feet, and on her head a crown of twelve stars". Pope Paul VI identified Our Lady with this woman in the opening words of his Apostolic Exhortation *Signum Magnum**, dated 12 May 1967: "The great sign which the Apostle John saw in Heaven, 'a woman clothed with the sun,' is interpreted by the sacred Liturgy, not without foundation, as referring to the most Blessed Mary, the Mother of all men by the grace of Christ the Redeemer." These words were addressed to the Catholic world on the eve of the Holy Father's pilgrimage to Fatima to commemorate the golden jubilee of the apparitions. And at the 1971 International Seminar at Fatima, Cardinal (then Fr.) Ciappi, O.P., papal theologian, repeated this conviction: "The apocalyptic image of the woman glowing with the sun's light may well be applied to the person of the Mother of God, seen by the beloved apostle as crowned with twelve stars and at the same time crying as she laboured in birth." (Apoc. 12:2).

The chapter goes on to relate how a "huge red dragon" appeared and threatened to devour the new-born child of the woman clothed with the sun. The woman fled into the wilderness where God had prepared a refuge for her, while the dragon continued to persecute the rest of her children who obey God's commandments and bear witness for Jesus. (Apoc. 12:17). This passage could easily relate to the great persecution of the Church foretold by Our Lady on 13 July 1917. A formidable enemy of God would rise up in Russia "and spread its errors throughout the world, raising up wars, revolutions and persecutions against the Church." The flight of the woman clothed with the sun would correspond to this persecution (which is unquestionably the severest in Church history). Ultimately the power of God would prevail. "In the end, my Immaculate Heart will triumph."

Alluding to this theme, Abbé André Richard, D.D., of Paris wrote in the January-February 1979 edition of *Soul* magazine: "As

---

*These two words (from Apoc. 12:1) form the opening for the introit of the Mass of the Assumption.

a professional philosopher, what I find most remarkable in the event of Fatima is that it is a heavenly intervention in the history of mankind in order to redirect history. Fatima is . . . an intervention to change the march of the entire caravan of mankind, which is on the road to a precipice over which it would inevitably fall unless its route is changed. Fatima concerns not only the pious Christian, but the man in the street — every man in the world. And as a theologian, what impresses me about Fatima is its reaffirmation of the entire gospel and its emphasis on the source of moral evil: offences against God which today mount even to the ultimate offence of militant atheism . . . How can any of us fail to be conscious of Our Lady appearing in the sky, reminding us of the great sign in chapters 11 and 12 of the Apocalypse? How can any of us consider Fatima to be less than the presentation of that apocalyptic message of Our Lady, dressed with the sun and announcing her triumph over the dragon?"

Several years earlier, Fr. Louis Kondor, S.V.D., a noted theologian and vice-postulator of the causes of Francisco and Jacinta, expressed the same conviction in the July-August 1975 edition of his regular bulletin, *Seers of Fatima.* "In view of this similarity, which seems a telling fulfillment of Apocalypse 12, who would venture any longer to speak of a private revelation? Fatima is . . . an eschatological sign that reveals the saving victory of the 12th chapter of the Apocalypse." He adds: "Vatican Council II spoke much of charisms and of the prophetic mystery of the Church. Relying on these words of the Church, we can consider Fatima as the great eschatological sign given by God to our times, so that we will not deserve the rebuke that Our Lord made to the Jews: 'You know how to read the face of the sky, but you cannot read the signs of the times.' (Matt. 16:4). Fatima is a sign of the times. The lightning flash that preceded each of Mary's apparitions at Fatima is an announcement of the lightning that will flash from east to west before the coming of the Son of Man. (Matt. 24:27). And the remaining atmospheric phenomena which belong to the complexity of Fatima are a presage of those signs in the sun, in the moon and in the stars that Our Lord speaks of in His eschatological discourse. (Luke 21:25). Fatima is a great sign of the times."

Yet despite these ominous portents, it would be wrong to view Fatima in an exclusively foreboding light. The great promise of the ultimate triumph of the Kingdom of God is a dazzling sign of hope for a tormented and fearful world. By this wondrous pledge, God manifests His unwearying love and concern for His wayward children. Though much of the world has abandoned Him, He has not abandoned the world. He reveals Himself through His Mother and promises to withhold the terrible arm of His Justice and forgive His rebellious sons, if a "sufficient number" correspond with His grace and return to His waiting arms like the Prodigal Son. He assures us of final reconciliation and peace. But having given us our free wills, he expects us to correspond with the grace of His message to attain that consummation so devoutly to be wished without having to be purified through suffering.

Our Lady relays these words to us "with an indescribable sadness and tenderness", pleading as only a mother can plead for her children in peril. She intercedes powerfully on our behalf, displaying that maternal love and care which we spoke of earlier, and which Vatican II expressed in *Lumen Gentium,* 62. "For taken up to Heaven, she did not lay aside this saving role, but by her manifold acts of intercession, continues to win for us gifts of eternal salvation. By her maternal charity, Mary cares for the brethren of her Son who still journey on earth, surrounded by dangers and difficulties." But she relies on our co-operation. "If people do what I ask, many souls will be saved and there will be peace." As the Communion of Saints teaches, she expects us to work for the salvation of sinners, for all men are brothers in Christ.

These themes were well developed by Cardinal Baggio, Prefect of the Congregation of Bishops, before 700,000 pilgrims at Fatima on 13 May 1976. "Still more evident and impressive is the relationship of the message of Fatima with the historical and theological reality of the happenings of Eden and Calvary . . . The evil which breaks loose and the infinite goodness of God Who does not let Himself be overcome by its insolent challenges; the expiation of the guilty and of the innocent which enters into God's plan in contrast with the implacable aggression of sin; the solidarity of all men under the Fatherhood of God Who makes us all brothers and Who, in His mercy, saves us in a marvellous succession of events from the first Adam to Christ and from the first Eve to the new Eve, Mary; the dialogue of love and pardon which rises above the cruelty, betrayal and mockery which are unleashed against the Just One; the hope and peace which spring forth from humiliation, sacrifice and pain in the two facets of the paschal mystery, the cross and the resurrection — all these are universal and eternal themes which the apparitions of Our Lady of Fatima, her revelations, her counsels and her confidences to the three children, have offered once again to the men of our century in a language as humble and popular as it is persuasive and moving. For over fifty years they have inspired meditation, prayer, penance, conversion, renewal of life. They have given rise to piety, charity, abnegation, a service and goodness at times truly heroic. They have infused consolation and joy. They have awakened the consciousness of ecclesial communion and of human solidarity in innumerable hosts of devoted people and pilgrims . . . especially among the poor and the suffering who feel an irresistible attraction."

In view of all this, one would surely expect the message of Fatima to be a matter of privileged priority in the Church today, as many prelates have stressed. "Do you believe in Fatima?" Pope Pius XII asked a group of American pilgrims led by Fr. Leo Goode in late August 1958. When they answered in the affirmative, His Holiness asked: "Will you do what Our Blessed Lady asked at Fatima?" On hearing their assent, the Holy Father stated: "If we are to have peace, we must all obey the requests made at Fatima. The time for doubting Fatima is long passed. It is now time for action."

But, one may ask with respectful concern: where do we see this action on anything like a national scale? Why are we not hearing the message of Fatima proclaimed loudly and clearly and repeatedly as the world lurches deeper into the black mire of iniquity and the threat of a global holocaust seems to advance each year? Said Bishop Graber of Regensburg a few years ago: "Is it not our fault that we, who are entrusted with the office of sentinels, have not raised our voice to preach the message over and over again?" He went on to quote from Ezekiel 33. "When I send a sword against a country, the people of that country select one of themselves and post him as a sentry: if he sees the sword coming against the country, he sounds his horn to alert the people. If someone hears the sound of the horn, but pays no attention, the sword will overtake him and destroy him; he will have been responsible for his own death. He has heard the sound of the horn and paid no attention; his death will be his own responsibility. But the life of someone who pays attention to the warning will be secure. If, however, the sentry has seen the sword coming, but has not blown his horn, and so the people are not alerted and the sword overtakes them and destroys one of them, the latter shall indeed die for his sin, but I will hold the sentry responsible for his death . . ."

He continued: "In the pamphlet *The Mission of a Bishop,* published by the Archiepiscopate of Cologne, there are two articles — 'the Prophetic Mission of a Bishop' and 'the Mission of Sentinel or Director' issued by the Secretariat of the Cologne Archiepiscopate. Here, instead of Ezekiel, Jonas is quoted. Jonas received an order from God to go to Nineve, the great city where he was to preach 'because their wickedness had become known to Him.' (1:2). What did the prophet do? He fled from the sight of the Lord. He did not want to preach, but only to say, as happens everywhere nowadays, what is flattering to the ear, what is pleasing; as St. Paul says (2 Tim. 4:3), 'what is pleasing, attractive and enticing', as a parochial bulletin stated recently.

"This censure for having abandoned the prophetic mission of vigilance falls on all of us. Because, like Jonas, we have refused to take on this mission, this storm has come upon us, as happened to Jonas. This is the storm that the Holy Father spoke of in his moving discourse of 29 June 1972, when he referred to the smoke of Satan that has penetrated through cracks in the structure of the Church . . . Ought we not to think seriously on the manner of uniting and utilising more perfectly the Marian associations and communities in Germany and other countries, so that they can have an active and decisive voice in the internal crisis of the Church? We do not want to remain settled and inactive, even while seeing how these destructive forces are calmly operating in the Church. We want to sound the trumpet energetically, to rouse those who are sleeping, to save our souls and those of our neighbours, and not fall into that sin of which Ezekiel speaks. If not, what will happen to us, to us who have been chosen as guards, who ought to broadcast Mary's exhortations and warnings? Having read what was spoken by the prophet Ezekiel, Chapter 33, about the sentry, we continue with verse 21: 'In the twelfth year of our captivity, a fugitive arrived from Jerusalem and said to me: The city has been taken.' Then, what will be said of us?"[2]

Bishop Graber's reference to what is "pleasing, attractive and enticing" could apply to the inroads of Modernism in the Church, the frequent relegation of Hell, Purgatory, penance and prayer, and the priority too often accorded to certain aspects of social and political action to the neglect of the spiritual. "Within the Church," says Karl Rahner, S.J., "there is to be found an exclusive commitment to temporal realities, which is not a legitimate choice, but apostacy and total loss of faith."[3] Our Lord gave a decisive answer to those who act thus: Without Me, you can do nothing . . . If you dwell in Me and My words dwell in you, ask what you will and you shall have it.

This watering down of the primacy of the spiritual purpose of life, in direct contradiction to Vatican II and the Magisterium, is probably the foremost reason for the alarming rise in lapsation from the Faith, the crisis in vocations, the emptying confessionals, the diminution of the sense of the sacred, irreverence towards the Blessed Sacrament and of particular concern, the widespread abandonment of the Forty Hours devotion at a time when sin is enthroned as never before and the need for Eucharistic reparation is consequently greater than ever. Said Dr. Graber at the 6th Congress of the Friends of Fatima, Freiburg, Germany, on 22 September 1973:

"Fatima is a judgement of God on a Church that thinks it can get along without prayer and penitence. Fatima is a judgement on a mini-style Christianity, with its low price and its liabilities growing apace."

Side by side with this spiritual malaise has come the insidious attack on many of the fundamental doctrines of the Church. Responsible theologians pontificate their home-bred dogmas which deceive, sow doubt and lead astray. From the benefit of hindsight, we can now see that the Fatima revelations were also intended by a merciful God to strengthen the Rock of Peter in anticipation of the present violent assault.

The angel's prayer of 1916: "My God, I believe, I adore, I hope, I love Thee; I ask pardon for those who do not believe, nor adore, nor hope, nor love Thee," is an affirmation of the three theological virtues of faith, hope and charity. It is also a wonderfully concise answer to the second question of the catechism: Why did God make you? (He made me to know Him, to love Him and to serve Him in this world, and to be happy with Him forever in the next.) The prayer further underlines our responsibility for the salvation of others, which we shall be considering more fully later.

The second apparition of the angel stressed the need for prayer and sacrifice — the fundamental precepts urged by Christ. "Pray always . . . Unless you take up your cross and follow Me, you cannot be My disciple . . . The Kingdom of Heaven suffereth violence and the violent bear it away." The angel also indicated how we were to make sacrifices. "Make everything you do a sacrifice. Above all, accept and bear with submission all the sufferings which the Lord may send you." This is a reminder of the most important undertaking we are called upon to do in life — the fulfillment of our daily spiritual duty and the acceptance of the trials and difficulties encountered each day in a spirit of humble submission to the Will of God.

In the autumn of 1916, the angel displayed the prayerful and profound reverence we should adopt towards the Blessed Sacrament, Which is Christ reigning in our midst in all the tabernacles of the world. It is worth noting that the sin of indifference towards the Eucharist (which some may not regard as a sin at all), is placed on a level with blasphemy and outrage. The angel also stressed the Real Presence of Christ in the consecrated Bread and Wine, which certain theologians question or explain away in terms of obscure phraseology.

The apparitions of Our Lady in the following year again emphasise the priority of penance and prayer, particularly the devout daily recitation of the gospel prayer of the rosary "which contains all the mysteries of our salvation," as Pope Leo XIII pointed out.[4] Also confirmed in Our Lady's appearances were the doctrine of the Holy Trinity, the Sacrifice of the Mass, the authority of the Pope, the existence of Heaven, Purgatory and Hell, of saints and demons that the Modernists try to eliminate, the meaning and value of suffering, the evil of sin and the serious obligation of every committed Christian to the work of atonement, the necessity of interior conversion, the indwelling of God in the souls of the just by grace, the mystery of Christ's redemption, the unique role of Mary as our Mediatrix with Christ, the importance of devotion to the Sacred Hearts of Jesus and Mary, the practice of the virtues and the spiritual and corporal works of mercy and so on. Even the doctrine of original sin is implied at Fatima, for the Immaculate Heart of Mary, which Fatima underlines, clearly brings into focus the Immaculate Conception which in turn points to the doctrine of the Fall.

In a message to all the world's priests, Cardinal Larraona, legate of Pope John XXIII at Fatima, declared on 13 May 1963:

"Upon us, dear brothers, falls the responsibility of administering to souls the inexhaustible treasures and spiritual riches of the message of Fatima. Fatima is a living realisation of the gospel recalled to us here by the Mother of God . . . Indeed, never has there been a supernatural manifestation of Our Lady of such rich spiritual content as that of Fatima, nor has any recognised apparition given us a message so clear, so maternal, so profound . . . Dear priests, I wish to exhort you anew to a profound penetration of the spiritual richness of the message Our Lady has confided to us and to engage yourselves with tenderness to conserve it always pure and integral in the souls of the faithful. Live and cause it to be lived . . ."

The most important aspects of the Fatima message are, as we have seen, prayer and penitence. They echo like a constant refrain through the words of the angel and Our Lady. And since they were accorded this emphasis, we need first to understand why this was so and how they become instrumental in transforming our lives and that of society as a whole. In this regard, we can do no better than recount the words of the Bishop of Fatima when he addressed the 8th Congress of the Friends of Fatima at Fulda, Germany on 21 September 1975. During this Congress, Cardinal Döpfner of Munich, President of the German Episcopal Conference, discussed with the various Marian organisations present the theme: Renewal of the cult and devotion to Our Lady, orientated by the Hierarchy, in the light of the Magisterium of the Church and of the message of Fatima. The Bishop's address, which was one of the highlights of this great Congress, is quoted at length on account of its exceptional value in analysing the key elements of the message: prayer and penitence.

"If we observe attentively the spiritual panorama of our days, within and without the Church, and confront it with the message of Fatima, we will see that it is an anticipated answer to the problems posed by men today, to Christians today. Inebriated by the conquests of science and technology, man has become alienated from God, secularised, rejecting all that is transcendent and supernatural.

"Fatima, from the first apparitions of the angel in the spring of 1916, to those of Our Lady in 1917 and the consequent heroic lives of the seers, is entirely an explosion of the divine. The Christian today lives in a state of perplexity and confusion, not only in view of the evils of the world, but also because of the disquiet that exists in the bosom of the Church herself, shaken as it is so deeply by the winds of heresy and disobedience. For we are witnessing the most radical negation of truths that were always part of the doctrinal patrimony of the Catholic faith, and an evident contempt for the authority of the Pope and the venerable pastors. Fatima is a proclamation of the faith for the Christian of today. If there is not a single article of the Creed that has not been questioned today, neither is there a truth of faith that Fatima has not reaffirmed. Fatima as a whole is a compendium of the Catholic faith, and the announcement of the gospel to the world of today. Fatima is a call to unity in obedience and in love . . .

"The cry of Fatima, a cry of penitence, constantly repeated, endeavours to save man in his frantic rush along the broad road of having, of unbridled enjoying, that leads fatally to the abyss of non-being. 'What are you doing?' This interpolation of the angel in the second apparition in the summer of 1916, takes on a prophetic character. It is directed, in the person of the little shepherds, to all humanity, to each man in particular, to you and me. It is an invitation to return to our interior home, to the most intimate depths of our inner selves, there where the great transfigurations are accomplished. As a preliminary to our return to God, comes this encounter with our own selves, like that related in the gospel parable of the Prodigal Son. 'He entered into himself.' (Luke 15:17). It was then that he recognised his tattered condition, his wasted self, and this saving decision sprang up within him: 'I will arise and go to my father.'

"The apparitions of the angel produced immediately in the seers a compelling need for silence, a factor still more marked after the apparitions of Our Lady. The message of Fatima invites modern man to this encounter with himself, to this personal reconciliation. It invites him to re-discover his identity as a human person, in the zone of silence which illuminates and transforms, that vital space, so to speak, of humanity restored in Christ, Who was also a Man of silence, in the desert, on the mountain and in the midst of the multitude. There must be a restoration of the love of silence, a creative silence, a saving silence, if we do not want man to be shattered and destroyed. Fatima is truly the symbol of the lone mountain, the contemplative wilderness, where every man should spend a while if he seriously wishes to avoid his own annihilation and to be fulfilled in the plenitude of his being.

"Reconciliation of man with himself is nothing more than the threshold and condition for reconciliation of man with God. The silence of Fatima, a silence so desired by the little shepherds, is a call to encounter with God in grace and love. This is the first and deepest meaning of the word penance in the message of Fatima, the anguished cry of the Mother delivered from the skies of the Cova da Iria to all the children of the Church and to all humanity. It is the great return to God of pilgrim humanity, of good, of love, of truth and of peace. Fatima has sounded the call of universal metanoia, interior conversion, renewal, recreation, and the transfiguration of the sons of men into children of God. For this, what is needed above all is that man recover the sense of sin. It is evident that he has lost it.

"Fatima discovers for us the true sense of sin; sin as an offence against God, as a negation of love, of adoration, of faith and of hope . . . The idea of the offence made to God by sin was engraved forever on the children's minds, and it was this that prompted them to make so many sacrifices as reparation and expiation. They wanted 'to console Our Lord'. 'Does He still remain so sad,' Francisco would say. 'I am so sorry that He is sad like this.'

"In the message of Fatima, sin exacts a temporal suffering that must be undergone on earth or in Purgatory, or eternal punishment for those who die as enemies of God . . . For the whole of their lives, the little seers made sacrifices for the conversion of sinners, in expiation and reparation, and in satisfaction for the sins of men.

"Reconciliation with God in the message of Fatima supposes, above all, that rupture with sin which is a personal attitude of man before the Lord and God his Father. It requires, then, souls in grace. It helps us to discover the meaning of a genuine Christian community. We can only have a Christian community in the measure that we have souls in grace, who possess supernatural life. This is fundamental. It is a lesser matter to organise great external solemnities and pilgrimages; it is not enough to have our churches full of people. If they are not in grace, then our churches are morgues and our parishes cemeteries.

"The great objective of the message of Fatima . . . is the resurrection of all the dead, the conversion of all Christians and of all men to the love of the Father; that all men may become the children of God and that all the children of God may be faithful to this Divine filiation that brings with it a vocation of love which means a permanent adherence to the adorable will of the Father, revealed in great things or in infinitely small ones, in the

Commandments and precepts of the Church, in the duties of one's state, which can be difficult and monotonous at times, in the duty towards one's family and profession, in human relations, in the social and political area. He is unfaithful to the message who resigns himself to his sinful state, or who lives in grace spasmodically, who does not make an effort to persevere, who does not begin again. Fatima has emerged on man's path to make it a pathway of grace and of love for God and his brothers.

"Fatima has been, all through its history, this way of return to the shelter of the home, that is, I mean, a call and a response of personal conversion, of interior renewal, of amendment of life. This is the great miracle of Fatima, the miracle of the moral order, the resurrection of so many who have found new life there. If the silence of those confessionals could be broken, we would be amazed and delighted. Who has not witnessed the interminable lines of penitents who, patiently and even heroically, await day and night the moment of their reconciliation with the Lord beneath the maternal eyes of Mary, refuge of sinners, whose conversion was the very reason for her coming to these skies and these lands?

"In the spirit of the message of Fatima, reconciliation with God requires a life of prayer, prayer understood as a personal and intimate conversation with God. The holy mountain of Fatima is a symbol and a prophecy of a return to prayer, in an epoch in which the name and thought of God are removed entirely from public life and even from the life of the individual, because of a growing atheism that invades all and everything to penetrate the very souls of each one, to a greater or lesser degree. The prayer of the message is a gratuitous prayer, that is to say, disinterested, not seeking personal advantage; we find in it and at every moment, the prayer of supplication, but only for the conversion of sinners and for peace. The prayer of the message goes hand in hand with sacrifice. 'Offer prayers and sacrifices constantly to the Most High. In every way you can, offer sacrifices in reparation for the sins which offend Him, and in supplication for the conversion of sinners.' (Second apparition of the angel).

"Fatima is youthful, because it is austere, demanding, hard, good for ardent, generous souls who know no measure of calculation. We must reveal the true face of Fatima to youth today, portrayed in the heroic lives of the little seers who were lovers of Jesus and His most holy Mother. The message of Fatima calls men to the way of Love. But along a line that is markedly biblical, it helps human littleness by recalling the last things: death, judgement, eternity, Purgatory, Heaven, Hell. Now it has become necessary in this hour of secularisation, to recall these doctrinal elements of the message that are, as has been said, a synthesis of the gospel."

NOTES

1. Quoted in *Soul* magazine, January-February 1979.
2. cf. *Seers of Fatima*, January-February 1974.
3. cf. *Il Cuore della Madre*, January 1978.
4. Quoted in *Sign of her Heart* by John Haffert, (A.M.I. Press, Washington, N.J., U.S.A., p. 196) which examines the close relation between the rosary and the brown scapular.

VII

THE COLLEGIAL CONSECRATION

WE must now return to the events of 1917 and examine the decisive element of the message of Our Lady of Fatima. The story of the heroic lives of Francisco and Jacinta during their remaining months on earth has been told many times; we shall only summarise it here before passing on to the crucial subject of the consecration of Russia and the promised triumph of the Immaculate Heart of Mary.

After the miracle of the sun, the three children continued their long prayers and formidable penances, regardless of health considerations. Eventually a holy and sympathetic priest, Fr. Faustino, persuaded them to modify their excesses within the bounds of prudence. All the same, Francisco would spend long hours daily before the tabernacle "consoling the hidden Jesus" as he would say to his companions, while Jacinta would kneel in tears for hours on end, imploring God to save souls from the terrifying inferno of Hell. One day, Francisco went missing. There was a long, anxious search for him. Finally, Lucia found him lying face down behind a wall in the fields, as if in a trance. "Francisco!" she called, shaking him anxiously. "What are you doing?" The little boy gradually roused himself and with a far-away gaze murmured: "I've been thinking of God. I've been thinking of all the sins which make Him so sad. If only I could console Him." The boy had progressed a long way spiritually since 1916. From praying and sacrificing himself to convert sinners, he had risen higher to be deeply grieved by the effects of sin in the Heart of Christ and to seek to console Him.

In addition to their many sacrifices, the children had to contend with endless questions from incessant streams of visitors arriving from all over Portugal. Finally in December 1918, Francisco fell ill with Spanish influenza which was ravaging the country. Shortly after Jacinta fell victim to the same dread disease, which was to claim 20 million lives around the world. Francisco bore his suffering with the greatest fortitude and patience, striving to remain as cheerful as he could and reciting his rosary almost continually. At length he grew so weak, he confessed to his mother that he simply could not say it any more: "my head hurts so much and I get all mixed up," he murmured. Olimpia gently reassured him and told him to say it in his heart, "for Our Lady will hear you just the same." On another occasion he whispered to Lucia: "It will not be long now before Jesus will come and take me to Heaven and there I shall see God and console Him and love Him forever."

Finally he grew so weak that he could no longer wear the penitential rope he had worn tightly round his waist. "Here, take it and burn it before the doctor sees it," he stammered to Lucia. "I simply can't stand it any more." One night shortly after this, he was heard crying out in anguish for his first Communion. His father hurried to fetch the priest. Francisco then told everyone except Lucia to leave the room. When the door finally closed he said in a low voice: "I want you to think carefully now and try and remember if you have ever seen me commit a sin." Lucia pondered for a few moments and mentioned some childish faults. Francisco nodded sadly. "It is true," he admitted tersely. "Now go and ask Jacinta if she remembers seeing me commit a sin." A few minutes later came word from Jacinta's sick room of a few more childish failings. The little boy was almost in tears. "It is true," he said. "I have confessed these already, but I will confess them again. Maybe it is because of these sins that Our Lord is so sad." His gaze rose to the crucifix on the wall and in a voice of grief he added: "Even if I was not to die; even if I was to grow up and be a man, I will never commit sin again. I am so sorry." Then joining his hands he repeated the prayer Our Lady had taught him to recite after each decade of the rosary: "O my Jesus, forgive us our sins, save us from the fires of Hell, and lead all souls to Heaven, especially those most in need."

The priest arrived and heard the boy's confession. The following morning he received his first Communion lying down, for he was too weak even to sit up. A radiant smile suffused his pallid face. "Today I am happier than you are," he said to Lucia "for I have the hidden Jesus in my heart." As night fell he was heard to cry out: "Mother! Look at that beautiful light by the door!" After a few minutes he said: "Now I can't see it any more." The following day, 4 April 1919, after begging everyone's pardon for anything he may have done to offend them, he expired peacefully. His body was buried in quicklime as was the custom and when it was finally exhumed in 1952 for translation to the new Basilica of the Rosary, only his bones were found. But clutched in the remains of his fingers was his fifteen decade rosary. Even in death, little Francisco still clung to his rosary.

Meanwhile Jacinta was sinking fast, but like her brother, spent the time praying and offering up her sufferings with the greatest perseverance and fortitude. During this period her love of God and Our Lady seems to have risen to ecstatic heights. She never tired repeating: "My God I love Thee in thanksgiving for all the graces you have granted me. O my Jesus, I love Thee! Sweet Heart of Mary, be my salvation!" Once she said to Lucia: "If only I could put into everybody the fire that is burning within me that makes me love Jesus and Mary so much!" At other times she would sit for hours on end with her face buried in her little hands, thinking of Hell "and the war that is to come." Once Lucia gave her a picture of the Sacred Heart and though Jacinta thought it a very poor depiction, she would kiss it frequently saying: "After all, it is Him. I kiss His Heart because it's what I like best." She begged for a picture of the Immaculate Heart of Mary so as to keep the two together.

In December 1919 Our Lady appeared again to Jacinta and asked her whether she would like to convert more sinners. The child bravely and generously consented. Our Lady then told her she would have to go to a hospital in Lisbon and there suffer a great deal, that she was to offer her sufferings for the conversion of sinners and in reparation for the offences against the Immaculate Heart of Mary, and that finally she would die there all alone, but she was not to be afraid, for the Blessed Virgin would be with her continually and eventually come and take her to Heaven. At that time it seemed impossible that the sick child would go to Lisbon, but soon after a doctor arrived with Fr. Formigão and both advised her mother that everything possible should be done to try to save the child's life "to ensure that Our Lady had really wished to take her." This meant sending Jacinta to one of the best hospitals in Lisbon. Broken-hearted, Jacinta said goodbye to Lucia and prayed for the last time in the Cova da Iria. When she finished she said to her mother: "When Our Lady went away, she passed over those trees and afterwards she went into Heaven so quickly that I thought her feet would get caught."

During her first weeks in Lisbon, Jacinta was cared for in an orphanage by a certain lay sister known as Mother Godinho. It seems that Our Lady appeared to her several times there, telling her many things which gave the child a wisdom far beyond her years. Quoting the Mother of God, on some occasions she said: "The sins of the world are very great . . . If men only knew what eternity is, they would do everything in their power to change their lives . . . You must pray much for sinners and priests and religious; priests should concern themselves only with the things of the Church . . . Fly from riches and luxury: love poverty and silence; have charity, even for bad people . . . Confession is a sacrament of mercy and we must confess with joy and trust . . . Priests must be very pure. Disobedience of priests and religious to their superiors gravely displeases Our Lord . . . Many marriages are not of God and do not please Our Lord . . . Certain fashions

will be introduced which will give great offence to God . . . Let
men avoid greed, lies, envy, blasphemy, impurity . . . The Mother
of God wants more virgin souls bound by the vow of chastity . . .
Woe to women wanting in modesty . . . Never speak ill of anyone.
Never complain or murmur. Be very patient, for patience leads us
to Heaven . . ." She also revealed that Our Lady had said that
wars are a punishment for sin and added: "Our Lady can no longer
uphold the arm of her Divine Son which will strike the world. If
people amend their lives, Our Lord will even now save the world,
but if they do not, punishment will come."

On 2 February Jacinta was admitted to hospital and eight days
later she was operated on for a purulent pleurisy and had two ribs
removed with only a local anaesthetic. Despite the atrocious pain,
she never complained, but was heard to murmur repeatedly: "Now
you can convert many sinners Jesus, for I suffer so much." Those
who might object to an innocent child having to undergo such
dreadful suffering should bear in mind that Jacinta, having witnessed the horrific vision of Hell, was consumed by the value of
suffering willingly offered up on behalf of unrepentant sinners. She
was living on a supernatural frame of existence and seeing everything through the eyes of eternity. "The example given us by the
visionaries in response to the Fatima message is both touching and
instructive," stated Cardinal Larraona, Prefect of the Sacred Congregation of Rites, on 13 May 1965 at Fatima.

Jacinta died on 20 February 1920, all alone as Our Lady had
foretold. All that afternoon she had been heard wailing of the lost
in Hell and pleading with God to accept her pain as penance for
hardened sinners. When the night nurse found her dead, there
were tears of blood on her little cheeks. The news flew across
Lisbon and great numbers came to pay their respects in the
Church of the Angels. Everyone noticed an unearthly fragrance
emanating from the body so that not even the hardest sceptic
could doubt it.

Initially, Jacinta was buried at Ourém, but in 1935 her body was
transferred to the cemetery at Fatima to lie beside the mortal
remains of Francisco. When the coffin was opened on that
occasion, everyone was astonished to find the body well preserved,
despite the quicklime in which it had been buried. In 1951,
Jacinta's body was translated to the new Basilica of the Rosary,
still in a remarkable state of preservation. To this day, many
pilgrims kneeling at her tomb have detected a celestial fragrance
there.

Meanwhile, increasing crowds continued to flock to Fatima
giving Lucia no respite from incessant questionings. In 1918 the

diocese of Leiria (which incorporated the parish of Fatima) was restored and Dr. José Alves Correira da Silva was consecrated Bishop. One of his first tasks was to rescue Lucia from her besieging visitors by sending her away with her mother's consent under an assumed name to a convent school at Vilar, near Oporto, where she could grow up like a normal child. In 1925 she entered the Order of St. Dorothy at Tuy, just over the Spanish border.

On 3 May 1922, the Bishop of Leiria opened an official ecclesiastical enquiry into the apparitions and after seven years of exhaustive investigation, and having obtained the unanimous approval of every bishop in Portugal, His Lordship published his Pastoral Letter on the cult of Our Lady of the Rosary of Fatima in which he spelt out the facts of the apparitions and the reasons for his favourable decision, as we have seen earlier.

A vast pilgrimage of thanksgiving resulted, comprising over 300,000 pilgrims and presided over by Cardinal Cerejeira, Patriarch of Lisbon. The spectacular ceremony was climaxed by the solemn consecration of Portugal to the Immaculate Heart of Mary by all the bishops of Portugal. From then on the shrine and the numbers of pilgrims resorting thither mushroomed. When the terrible Spanish Civil War broke out in 1936, the Portuguese bishops implored Our Lady to protect their country. Their prayer being answered, some 500,000 pilgrims poured into the Cova da Iria with over 100 priests and 20 prelates on 13 May 1938, when the solemn consecration of the country to the Immaculate Heart of Mary was renewed in conjunction with the consecration of every parish in the entire country. It is highly significant that the sole diocese in Spain which had been similarly consecrated, that of Seville, was the only one left unscathed by the murderous Civil War, which claimed 2,000,000 casualties.

Meanwhile Lucia continued to receive visions: on the night of 10 December 1925 Our Lady appeared to her with the Child Jesus and asked for the reparatory devotion of the Five First Saturdays, which we shall examine at length when we analyse the cult of devotion and reparation to the Immaculate Heart of Mary. On 15 February 1926 the Child Jesus again appeared to Lucia and uttered those memorable words: "What is being done to establish devotion to the Heart of My Mother?" Lucia explained that while her superior was disposed to propagate the cult, the confessor said that she alone could do nothing. Our Lord answered: "It is true that your superior alone can do nothing, but with My grace she can do everything."

The following year Lucia was given permission by Our Lord to reveal the first part of the secret — that concerning devotion to the Immaculate Heart of Mary. Beginning in the convent at Pontevedra, the devotion spread throughout the country and overseas.

Fr. Formigão was one of the leading protagonists of the cult in Portugal. Meanwhile Lucia had been given permission to make a Holy Hour in the beautiful chapel of the community at Tuy, Spain, every week between 11 pm and midnight. And on 13 June 1929 she received the greatest of all her visions which was only made public in August 1967 after Pope Paul's visit to Fatima. It was a climatic vision of the Most Holy Trinity in which Our Lady came to fulfill her promise of 13 July 1917: "I shall come to ask for the consecration of Russia to my Immaculate Heart." The following is Lucia's own account of that sublime vision, which she wrote in 1931 on the order of her confessor.

"I had asked for and obtained permission from my superiors to make a Holy Hour from 11 pm to midnight during the night of Thursday-Friday. Being alone one night, I knelt down in the middle of the balustrade which is in the centre of the chapel to recite, prostrate, the prayers of the angel. Feeling tired, I got up and continued to recite them with arms outstretched. The only light was that of the sanctuary lamp. Suddenly the whole chapel lit up as by a supernatural light, and there appeared on the altar a cross of light which rose up as far as the ceiling. In this very clear light one could see on the upper part of the cross the figure of a man from the waist upwards and upon his chest was a dove, also luminous. Nailed to the cross was another man. A little below his waist, suspended in the air, one could see a chalice and a large host upon which there fell several drops of blood which flowed upon the cheeks of the crucified one and from a wound on his chest. Flowing over the host, these drops fell into the chalice.

"Under the right arm of the cross was Our Lady (it was Our Lady of Fatima with her Immaculate Heart in her left hand without sword or roses, but with a crown of thorns and flames). Under the left arm of the cross, large letters of crystalline water flowed down over the altar and formed these words: Grace and Mercy.[1] I understood that the mystery of the Most Holy Trinity had been shown to me and I received enlightenment upon this mystery which it is not permitted to me to reveal.

"Our Lady then said to me: 'The moment has come for God to ask the Holy Father to make, in union with all the bishops of the world, the consecration of Russia to my Immaculate Heart. He promises to save Russia by this means. There are so many souls that the justice of God condemns for sins committed against me, that I have come to ask for reparation. Sacrifice yourself for this intention and pray.' I gave an account of this to my confessor and he asked me to write down what Our Lord wanted to be done.

"Later on, through an intimate communication, Our Lord complained: 'They have not chosen to heed my request . . . As the King of France, they will regret it and then will do it, but it will be late. Russia will already have spread her errors throughout the world, provoking wars and persecutions against the Church. The Holy Father will have much to suffer.' "

This extraordinary vision eloquently summed up the salvific message of Fatima — Trinitarian, Eucharistic and Marian. As for the consecration of Russia to the Immaculate Heart of Mary by the Holy Father in union with all the world's bishops (known as the Collegial Consecration), Sister Lucia has insisted that it must be done "exactly as Our Lady requested." On 21 January 1935 she wrote to her confessor: "As for Russia, it seems to me that it will very much please Our Lord by working so that the Holy Father will achieve His designs. About three years ago Our Lord was very displeased because His request had not been attended to and I made this fact known to the Bishop in a letter. Until now, Our Lord has asked nothing more from me than prayers and sacrifices. From an intimate conversation with Him, it seems that He is ready to show mercy towards Russia as He promised five years ago and which He wishes so much to save."

In another letter dated 18 May 1936 she wrote: "About the other questions, if it will be convenient to insist in order to obtain the consecration of Russia? I answer in almost the same way as I answered in other times. I am sorry that it has not been done yet, but the same God Who asked for it is the One Who permitted it . . . It seems to me that if the Holy Father did it right now, God would accept it and would fulfill His promise; and without any doubt, through this act, the Holy Father would gladden Our Lord and the Immaculate Heart of Mary. Intimately, I have spoken to Our Lord about the subject and not too long ago I asked Him why He would not convert Russia without the Holy Father making that consecration. (He replied) 'Because I want My whole Church to acknowledge that consecration as a triumph of the Immaculate Heart of Mary so that it may extend its cult later on and put the devotion to the Immaculate Heart beside the devotion to My Sacred Heart.' 'But My God' (Lucia answered), 'the Holy Father probably will not believe me, unless You Yourself move Him with a special inspiration.' 'The Holy Father,' (Our Lord answered), 'pray much for the Holy Father. He will do it, but it will be late. Nevertheless, the Immaculate Heart of Mary will save Russia. It has been entrusted to her'."[2]

Meanwhile, attempts were being made from other quarters (principally by the Servant of God, Alexandrina da Costa)[3] for the consecration of the world to the Immaculate Heart of Mary, presumably as a first step towards the ultimate Collegial Consecration of Russia. In 1938 came the great light which warned Lucia of the imminence of the Second World War. When Germany invaded Poland, the Bishop of Fatima almost immediately proclaimed and recommended the devotion of reparation to the Immaculate Heart of Mary and implemented a campaign to propagate it throughout the country.

The following year Sister Lucia wrote to Pope Pius XII asking for the Collegial Consecration. However the diocesan authorities prevailed upon her to modify her request to the consecration of the world to the Immaculate Heart of Mary with a special mention of Russia, which they deemed far more likely to be executed by the Holy Father. Sister Lucia added in her revised draft that "Our Lord has promised to shorten the days of tribulation" if the consecration to the world is effected. Pope Pius XII finally complied with the request on 31 October 1942, the silver jubilee year of the apparitions and of his episcopal ordination.[4]

In the course of his broadcast to the world, the Holy Father said: "Queen of the Most Holy Rosary, Refuge of the human race, Victress in all God's battles, we humbly prostrate ourselves before thy throne, confident that we shall receive mercy, grace and bountiful assistance and protection in the present calamity, not through our own merits, but solely through the goodness of thy maternal Heart. To you, to your Immaculate Heart, We, as universal Father of the great Christian family, as Vicar of Him to Whom has been given all power over Heaven and earth, and from Whom we have received the care of all souls redeemed by His Blood, who inhabit the world; to you, to your Immaculate Heart, in this tragic hour of human history, we entrust, we offer, we consecrate, not only Holy Church, the Mystical Body of your Son Jesus, which suffers and bleeds in so many places and in so many ways, but also the whole world torn by mortal strife, ablaze with hate and victim of its own sins . . . Queen of Peace, pray for us and give to the world now at war the peace for which all people are longing — peace in the truth, justice and charity of Christ . . . Give peace to the peoples separated from us by error or by schism, and especially to those who profess such singular devotion to thee and in whose homes an honoured place was ever accorded thy venerable icon (today perhaps often kept hidden to await better days); bring them back to the one true fold of Christ under the one shepherd . . ."

A few days later came the turning point of the war according to Sir Winston Churchill.[5] The following month Sister Lucia wrote: "God has already shown His satisfaction with this act, although incomplete according to His wish, performed by the Holy Father and several bishops. He promises to end the war soon, but the conversion of Russia is not for now."

On 7 July 1952, in an Apostolic Letter *Sacro Vergente Ano,* Pope Pius XII consecrated Russia explicitly to the Immaculate Heart of Mary, though without the world's bishops participating. Sister

Lucia wrote shortly afterwards: "I thank you for the newspaper cutting reporting the consecration of Russia. I am grieved that it has not yet been carried out as Our Lady had asked. Patience! . . . Let us hope that Our Lady, as a good Mother, will be pleased to accept it."

In 1954 Pope Pius XII issued his encyclical *Ad Coeli Reginam*, in which he *commanded* that an act of consecration to the Immaculate Heart of Mary be made annually in every parish in the world on the feast of the Queenship of Our Lady. It seems that by this means, His Holiness was preparing for the eventual Collegial Consecration. Tragically, the Holy Father's request was largely ignored. Ten years later, immediately after the promulgation of the Dogmatic Constitution of the Church during Vatican II, Pope Paul VI renewed the consecration of the world to the Immaculate Heart of Mary in the presence of all the world's bishops, at the same time proclaiming Our Lady Mother of the Church and announcing a mission to Fatima. Yet even this singular act did not exactly fulfill the specific request of Our Lady of Fatima. According to Sister Lucia, God will only permit the grace of the Collegial Consecration "when a sufficient number are complying with the message of Fatima."

Over the years, several objections have been raised to the Collegial Consecration on political and theological grounds, the principle one being that the Pope cannot consecrate a people against their will.

The answer given by competent theologians is that the Collegial Consecration is indeed perfectly feasible due to the Communion of Saints. In any case, it is not a consecration of individuals, but of a nation as a whole. And even though the Russian Orthodox Church do not come under the authority of Rome, they certainly come under it morally, since Christ established one teaching authority for His Church.

In the past few years, some 500 bishops and 3,000,000 people have petitioned Rome for the Collegial Consecration. Explaining why it has not yet been attained, the renowned theologian and philosopher Abbé André Richard of Paris stated: "Ultimately, we must look for an answer in the Divine Will since the political and theological objections have been adequately answered." He also felt that lack of world-wide awareness would necessarily prevent the effect desired by Our Lord (in His words to Sister Lucia), namely that the whole world recognise that the promised change in Russia will have been obtained specifically through the Immaculate Heart of Mary after this consecration is made.[6]

One of Europe's foremost theologians, Dr. Joaquin Alonso of Madrid,[7] agreed with this view and added: "Certainly a prerequisite to the Collegial Consecration is world-wide individual

and diocesan acts of consecration which Pope Pius XII and subsequently Pope Paul VI have urged and even commanded."

(Dr. Alonso referred to *Ad Coeli Reginam* mentioned above and
Pope Paul's *Signum Magnum,* issued on 12 May 1967 on the day
before his pilgrimage to Fatima. In this important encyclical His
Holiness stated: "We now exhort all the sons of the Church to
renew personally their consecration to the Immaculate Heart of
the Mother of the Church.")

Elaborating on all this, Dr. Alonso explained that the ultimate
reason why the Collegial Consecration had not yet been effected
would seem to be "because the Holy Father does not judge it
opportune." He went on: "Before criticising the delay of the Pope,
it is necessary to consider the following:

1. Only the Pope knows all the circumstances which would make
   this consecration opportune. Furthermore, it is the same Pope
   who holds the supreme authority to judge on the message which
   any apparition — even when true — brings to the Church and
   to the world. He knows then, when and how it will be useful and
   convenient to make the consecration, as asked by Our Lady.

2. The consecration of Russia must not be understood as a
   mechanical recitation of some formula, but rather as a spiritual
   action taken by the Pope in union with all the bishops of the
   Catholic world, on the part of all Christianity, invoking the
   powerful intercession of the Immaculate Heart of Mary. The
   Pope has the authority for this in virtue of being the visible head
   of the entire Mystical Body which is the Church. It makes no
   difference that the Russian Christians do not also make the
   consecration, nor even that they be informed of it, because the
   communion in the Mystical Body of Christ is real and touches
   all Christians.

3. The decision of the Pope must be reached not only by a movement of petitions directed to him, but even more, by such a
   living of the message of Fatima that Our Lady obtains the grace
   for the Holy Father to make this consecration which will bring
   such great benefits to the Church and to the world. We can
   therefore say that in the hidden Providence of God it is to be
   hoped that firstly, we ourselves fully realise the consecration to
   the Heart of our Mother in Heaven; and secondly, to obtain
   from the Lord the grace of the Collegial Consecration of
   Russia.

   Therefore instead of being so preoccupied that the Holy
   Father make the consecration, let us intensify our apostolate
   for ourselves and others to live the message of Fatima fully. If
   we do, certainly we will obtain from the Lord this grace for the
   Church and for the world."

Dr. Alonso was asked for the meaning of Lucia's words: "The Pope will make the consecration of Russia, but it will be late." He replied: "This phrase of Lucia is certain. And from Lucia herself we have the following understanding of its meaning: 'The consecration of Russia and also the final triumph of the Immaculate Heart of Mary which will follow it, are absolute and will be realised despite all the obstacles.' However, according to that which we said above in answer to the first question, because we ourselves, through our sins, have not merited that the Pope should make the consecration, we are passing through a period of calamities which we would be able to shorten if we would be truly converted to the Lord. For this reason, it is 'too late' in order to free us from the evils through which we are now passing. However, it is never too late to obtain the ultimate grace from Our Lord if we demand it with a sincere heart."

Dr. Alonso was also asked whether the Pope could "demand" that the bishops join with him in making the consecration of Russia. He replied: "The Pope, in virtue of his supreme jurisdiction over the entire Church, both pastors and faithful, has the authority to demand all that refers to morality and good customs. The totality which is asked is not materially numerical but moral. That is to say, the major part. And this is an easy matter to accomplish." However since Vatican II opened a new era of collegiality, the Holy Father does not tend to act unilaterally, but would undoubtedly sound out the views of the episcopal conferences of the world before going ahead.

The Collegial Consecration is therefore the climactic act in the great drama of Fatima. But whether or not the final part of Our Lady's prophecy of 13 July 1917 concerning the "annihilation of various nations" is fulfilled before this consecration, depends, as we have seen, on whether a "sufficient number" comply with the Blessed Virgin's message of prayer and penance. Each of us should pray and sacrifice ourselves daily for this supreme intention. Among the several millions of petitions in recent years asking the Holy Father to implement the Consecration was that of Sister Lucia herself.

On 13 July 1974 during a Mass concelebrated by 100 priests in the Cova da Iria, the Bishop of Fatima stated: "How great is the mission that, by God's mandate, the Pope and all the bishops must discharge in the plans appointed by God for the world in which we live. Each of us should pray for the higher authorities in the Church and particularly for the bishop of his diocese, so that by this joint and communal action, the triumph of the Kingdom of God may be hastened through the promised triumph of the Immaculate Heart of Mary."

NOTES

1. In the liturgy of the Feast of the Sacred Heart we read: "Streams of grace and mercy flow from the opened Heart." From John 7: 37-39, it is clear that the water flowing from Christ's Heart is symbolic of the Holy Spirit, and from John 19: 31-37, the symbol of the Holy Spirit is seen sanctifying the sacrifice of the Lamb, signified by the Blood and Water.

2. cf. *Memoirs and Letters of Sister Lucia,* Martin's edition, 1973, page 415.

3. Alexandrina da Costa (whose cause for beatification is further advanced than that of Padre Pio) was an apparently genuine mystic living in northern Portugal whose mission paralleled that of Sister Lucia. cf. *Alexandrina: The Agony and the Glory,* by Francis Johnston, Veritas Publications, Dublin, 1979.

4. By an extraordinary coincidence, Pope Pius XII had been ordained bishop at the exact hour that Our Lady first appeared at Fatima, 13 May 1917.

5. cf. *The Second World War* by Sir Winston Churchill, Vol. 4, 33. The latter's exact words were "the turning of the hinge of fate."

6. The views of Dr. André Richard and Dr. Joaquin Alonso were reported in the January-February 1976 edition of *Soul* magazine, official organ of the Blue Army in America.

7. Dr. Alonso, C.M.F., of Spain, is considered one of the world's foremost authorities on Fatima. He obtained a doctorate in philosophy and theology from the Gregorian University, Rome, and has pursued further studies at Louvain, Heidelberg and the Sorbonne, in addition to teaching philosophy and theology at Rome, Madrid and Lisbon. He has been appointed by the Bishop of Fatima to prepare the critical and definitive study of Fatima and its message.

VIII

EUCHARISTIC REPARATION

WE now come to the most important part of this book: what is the precise meaning of Our Lady of Fatima's call for prayer and penance? Exactly what constitutes the Peace Plan from Heaven which the New Esther brings to a violent, degenerate world, and by means of which she can save it from self-destruction by her intercessory power with the King, who is her Son? According to Cardinal Larraona, former Prefect of the Sacred Congregation of Rites and Legate of Pope John XXIII at Fatima on 13 May 1963, the message of Our Lady is "an appeal from the Sorrowful and Immaculate Heart of Mary, inviting all to practice the eternal truths of the gospel . . . It contains the richest, most maternal, clear and profound message of all such that have been given to us down the centuries." Its characteristic notes are, according to the Bishop of Fatima in a 1967 pastoral letter: "evangelical simplicity, sound theology based on perennial tradition, perfect harmony with authentic asceticism and mysticism, strong and absolute union with the Pope and the Church, and deep interior devotion to Mary."

Certain aspects of the message, such as the daily rosary and sacrifice, were known even while the apparitions were in progress, but it was only after the publication of Lucia's Memoirs from 1935 to 1941 that the full implication of the message became realised. The underlying theme was identified as Eucharistic reparation. The tragic decline in the cult of Eucharistic devotion since Vatican II prompted the Blue Army of Our Lady of Fatima and other apostolates to dedicate themselves to rectifying this serious imbalance. Though great stress was certainly laid by the Council on the priority of the Mass, many inadvertently understood this to mean a de-emphasis of Eucharistic adoration. But the placing of tabernacles to one side of the Church was really intended by the Council Fathers to create special chapels of adoration. Pope Paul VI repeatedly emphasised this, especially in his beautiful encyclical *Mysterium Fidei* and in his message to the Eucharistic Congress at Philadelphia in August 1976.

That Eucharistic reparation is also a necessary prerequisite to living the Fatima message well was shown in the preparation given to the three children by the angel in 1916 and by Our Lady in her very first appearance the following year. The angel prostrated himself before the Blessed Sacrament and after reciting a sublime prayer of reparation "for the countless outrages, sacrileges and indifferences" committed against the Eucharist, he urged the children to "make reparation and console your God." Thereafter the children would spend many hours daily repeating this prayer, so that by the spring of 1917 they were well versed in the practice of Eucharistic reparation.

It is highly significant that the first apparition of the Blessed Virgin took place on 13 May 1917, Feast of Our Lady of the Blessed Sacrament. This title was called by Pope St. Pius X "the most theological of all Mary's titles after that of Mother of God."[1] When she opened her hands on the children and communicated to them streams of intense light, which overwhelmed their souls causing them to feel 'lost in God' Whom they recognised in that light, they threw themselves to the ground in adoration (just as the angel had taught them) and poured out their love of the Blessed Sacrament in a transport of praise.

To understand why Our Lady prepared the children in this extraordinary manner, we have to remember that her title Our Lady of the Blessed Sacrament not only reminds us that the greatest of all graces came to us through her, but that her life after the Ascension when she resided with St. John must have been a model of Eucharistic love and adoration which we should strive to imitate. The Acts of the Apostles tell us how "they were persevering . . . in the communication of the breaking of the bread." (Acts 2:42). This continuous Eucharistic life was the distinctive note of the primitive Church. In the catacombs, we find that the most common symbols etched by the first Christians were those of the Eucharist and Our Lady. During her remaining years on earth, the Blessed Virgin must have been particularly drawn to the Blessed Sacrament. "She found again in the adorable Host the blessed fruit of her womb," says St. Peter Julian Eymard, "and in her life of union with the Eucharist, the happy days of Bethlehem and Nazareth. Mary it was, indeed, who above all the rest, must have persevered in the breaking of the bread. Hence she is the model of Eucharistic adorers. She ascended Calvary, but she returned with her adopted son St. John to begin in the Cenacle her new maternity at the feet of Jesus in the Eucharist."[2]

Today, as mother of mankind, her task is to train her children (subject of course to their co-operation), into accepting the reality of her Divine Son in the Eucharist and the serious obligation that this truth imposes on us. In opening her hands on the three children and pouring forth that intense Eucharistic light, she was repeating in a mystical manner (and at the same time reminding us of) the moment when she first opened that furrow of fire in Bethlehem which was to sweep across the world. The flesh which she gave Him was the same flesh with which He glorified His Father, redeemed us, and nourishes us today with the Bread of Life. Hence it is clear that devotion and reparation to the Eucharist, especially when made through the magnifying lens of the Immaculate Heart of Mary, is a very necessary and powerful means of preparing ourselves to live the Fatima message really well. A dramatic embodiment of this truth is seen during the night vigils at Fatima on the 12th of May to October in preparation for the celebrations on the 13th, when many thousands remain on their knees for hours before the Blessed Sacrament exposed, some with imploring arms outspread, mindless of the chill mountain air, wind or rain. They have taken the message of Fatima to their hearts and are living it intensely. As the Bishop of Fatima characterised the message: *Reparation. Reparation. Reparation. Especially Eucharistic reparation.*

The greatest form of Eucharistic reparation we can possibly make to God is the offering of the sacrifice of the Mass, which is the projection through time and space of the one supreme sacrifice of Calvary. This was the essence of the climatic vision at Tuy in 1929 — the offering of Christ crucified to the Eternal Father in satisfaction for our sins, both on Calvary and in its mystical continuation which is the Mass (the latter being signified in the vision by the host dripping blood into the chalice). In the words of the Council of Trent: "In order to effect our eternal salvation, Christ willed to sacrifice Himself once to the Father upon the altar of the cross. But His Priesthood was not to cease at His death. Therefore at the Last Supper, He offered His Body and Blood in the form of bread and wine, thus bequeathing to His Church a sacrifice through which the sacrifice of the Cross, once offered, is made present, its memory preserved until the end of the world, and His healing power applied to us for the remission of sins which we daily commit." *(Doctrina de S.S. Missae Sacrificio,* Ci).

Since we unite ourselves to the gifts offered at Mass (symbolised by the mingling of water with the wine at the Offertory to represent all the participants present), and since at the Consecration the bread and wine are transubstantiated into the Body and Blood of Christ, we make the sacrifice of Calvary our very own by offering ourselves to the Father in union with our Redeemer. This is to say, we offer up to God the satisfaction for sin gained by Christ on Calvary as satisfaction for our sins and the sins of others. Though all men were potentially redeemed by Calvary, the free co-operation of each person is essential for the actualisation and the application of that redemption. This is the most compelling reason for our frequent participation at Mass —

to apply the merits of the mystical sacrifice to millions of others in this age of rampaging sin.

The Eucharist is not only a sacrifice; it is also, of course, Communion. In the words of Pope John Paul II in *Redemptor Hominis:* "The Eucharist is a Sacrifice-sacrament, a Communion-sacrament and a Presence-sacrament." As a Communion-sacrament It is the food and strength of our souls. "Jesus took the bread and blessed and broke It and gave It to His disciples saying, Take and eat, this is My Body." (Matt. 26:26). Then He took the cup and offered thanks and gave it to them saying, "Drink this all of you, for this is My Blood of the new testament, shed for many to the forgiveness of sins." (Matt. 26: 27-28). Through eating the Bread of Life, we receive the greatest share of the graces acquired for us at Calvary which flow from the altar at Mass. Not only do we gain essential nourishment for our souls, but we acquire a personal and intimate relationship with Christ: we live *in* Him, *with* Him and *by* Him; and through Him with the Father and the Holy Spirit. "He who eats My Flesh and drinks My Blood lives always in and with Me, and I in and with him." (John 6:57). It is important to note that the host seen dripping blood in both the third apparition of the angel and the 1929 apparition at Tuy underlines the truth that Christ is received wholly and entirely under either species.

The need for Communions of reparation was particularly stressed by the angel in 1916. "Receive the Body and Blood of Our Lord Jesus Christ, horribly outraged by ungrateful men. Make reparation and console your God." The angel was referring to sacrilegious Communions, the desecration of tabernacles and violation of consecrated hosts which occur with chilling frequency throughout the world. Medieval Catholics used to build churches in expiation on the site of the latter sacrilege, but times seem to have changed — or more likely, there would now be too many churches to build . . .

Besides these heinous crimes, there is the lapsation of millions of our fellow Catholics to atone for. We bear a serious responsibility for their salvation in the Mystical Body of Christ. Finally, we must make amends for the growing contagion of unnecessary Sunday work which constitutes a grave sin in the eyes of God. The great mystic Père Lamy[3] revealed that repeated violation of the third commandment was one of the three causes of the First World War (the others being blasphemy and the desecration of marriage). "Keeping Sunday holy," he had foretold in 1925, "is what will save England from invasion during the next world war."

The finest way in which we can expiate these heartless affronts to God's love is by participating at extra Sunday and weekday Masses and receiving Communion as frequently as possible in a spirit of reparation. Even when she was quite ill, little Jacinta would drag herself along the lengthy country lanes to daily Mass in the parish church at Fatima, answering Lucia's pleas for restraint with "I'm going for sinners who don't even go to Mass on Sundays." If a sick child can do it, we certainly can. Forcing oneself to give up that warm fire, that comfortable armchair, that favourite TV programme, that evening of legitimate leisure, to participate in an extra Mass and receive Communion regardless of weariness or weather — this is the ultimate response that the message of Fatima requires of all committed Catholics today.

Exceptional times demand exceptional conduct. The wave of evil today can only be turned back by a counter-wave of holiness, as the Bishop of Fatima has said. "We are all called upon to participate in the work of expiation," said Pope Paul VI in *Poenitentiam Agite.* The opportunity is now and will shortly disappear forever. We must be "either hot or cold". (Apoc. 3:16). "We cannot be half a saint," insisted St. Thérèse of Lisieux (who was the "greatest saint of modern times", according to Pope St. Pius X), "we must be a whole saint, or no saint at all." Or as the Archbishop of Freiburg, Germany, expressed it on 22 September 1973 at the 6th Congress of the Friends of Fatima: "No one has a right to be mediocre at this critical hour." And underlining this crying need to Cardinal Luciani (the future Pope John Paul I) on 11 July 1977, Sister Lucia spoke with great energy and conviction on the necessity for priests, religious and Christians "with strength of mind, who must be as radical as the saints. It must be all or nothing if they want to belong seriously to God," she stressed.[4]

The Eucharistic thrust of the Fatima message also embraces the cult of adoration of the Blessed Sacrament. We have seen that the angel taught the children how to adore God in the Host; later, Our Lady asked Jacinta to request a chapel of perpetual adoration in the Cova da Iria. Today, this chapel stands a few yards from the spot where Our Lady appeared.

Long before 1917 however, Our Lord had asked St. Margaret Mary for one hour of adoration before the tabernacle every month. Over the years, the cult of the Holy Hour as it became known, spread all over the world and developed into the Forty Hours devotion. Though widely discarded in many areas since Vatican II (which, as we have noted, was contrary to the teaching of the Council and of Pope Paul VI), the cult of Eucharistic adoration is again increasing, mainly as a result of the unwearying devotion of the Blue Army and several other Fatima apostolates, which have responded with great zeal to the anguished cry of the Saviour in Gethsemane: 'Could you not watch one hour with Me?' Their reply has been the all-night vigil of reparation before the Blessed Sacrament exposed.

The prostration of the angel before the Eucharist and the

fervour of his sublime reparatory prayer also remind us of the profound reverence we should display before the tabernacle — respectful genuflection and posture, interior recollection, bowing one's head at the name of Jesus (as Pope Gregory X commanded)[5], and the cessation of idle chatter in Church (something that Jacinta used to frown upon). For we are in the presence of the same Christ before whom the angels and saints prostrate themselves in Heaven crying out: Holy, Holy, Holy, Lord God of Hosts, Heaven and earth are full of Thy glory, Hosanna in the highest.

"It is our loving duty to honour and adore the Blessed Bread which we see with our eyes," declared Pope Paul VI in his *Credo of the People of God*, "the Word Incarnate Himself made present before us." And in his beautiful encyclical *Mysterium Fidei*, the same pontiff wrote: "The Catholic Church has always offered and still offers the cult of *latria* to the sacrament of the Eucharist, not only during Mass, but also outside of it, reserving consecrated Hosts with the utmost care, exposing them to solemn veneration, and carrying them processionally to the joy of great crowds of the faithful. In the ancient documents of the Church, we have many testimonials of this veneration . . .

"In the course of the day, the faithful should not omit to visit the Blessed Sacrament, which according to the liturgical laws, must be kept in the churches with great reverence in a most honourable location. Such visits are a proof of gratitude, an expression of love, an acknowledgement of the Lord's presence.

"No one can fail to understand that the Divine Eucharist bestows upon the Christian people an incomparable dignity. Not only while the sacrifice is offered and the sacrament is received, but as long as the Eucharist is kept in our churches and oratories, Christ is truly the Emmanuel, that is, *God with us*. Day and night He is in our midst, He dwells with us, full of grace and truth (cf. John 1:14). He restores morality, nourishes virtues, consoles the afflicted and strengthens the weak. He proposes His own example to those who come to Him, that all may learn to be, like Himself, meek and humble of heart and seek not their own interests, but those of God.

"Anyone who approaches this august sacrament with special devotion and endeavours to return generous love for Christ's own infinite love, will experience and fully understand — not without joy and fruit — how precious is the life hidden with Christ to God (cf. Col. 3:3) and how great is the value of converse with Christ; for there is nothing more consoling on earth, nothing more efficacious for advancement along the road to salvation."

Echoing the words of His Holiness, the Bishop of Honolulu wrote to all priests in his diocese at the beginning of 1979, stressing the importance of the Fatima message and adding: "The need for such dedication of our people to the Blessed Sacrament and to the devotions contained therein are now paramount."

Today, we seem to be living in an age of unprecedented Eucharistic manifestations, as if God was going to exceptional lengths to bring home to us the importance of what has been recounted above. There is the incorrupt body of St. Charbel Makhlouf, the great modern saint of the Mass, which is still perspiring a mixture of blood and water; the Eucharistic fasts of Berthe Petit and Alexandrina, to name just two in this century, and the sublime miracle of Lanciano. The case of Alexandrina is especially important since her fourteen year sustenance on the Eucharist alone was confirmed in hospital by the highest medical authorities as "scientifically inexplicable." She was reputedly told by Christ: "You are living on the Eucharist alone because I wish to prove to the world the power of the Eucharist and the power of my life in souls."[6]

In 1971, medical science was able to verify one of the very greatest Eucharistic miracles of all time. The story began 1,200 years ago when a certain Basilian monk in Lanciano, Chieli, Italy, who doubted the Divine Presence in the Host after the consecration at Mass, was astounded to see it visibly change into flesh, except in the centre where the appearance of the sacramental species remained intact. The consecrated wine changed into blood, coagulating into five small clots. The host-flesh remains to this day, enclosed in a finely wrought silver monstrance dating back to 1713. The blood is kept in a crystal chalice fixed to the monstrance base.

Over the centuries there have been four official investigations by ecclesiastical authorities. The latest and by far the most searching was undertaken in November 1970 at the request of the Holy See, and the aid of medical science was enlisted to establish once and for all the reality of the apparent prodigy or otherwise. The investigating committee set up comprised renowned laboratory researchers in the medical field chosen from universities in Siena, Florence and Turin and headed by Professor Edward Linoli, chief of the medical staff of research and one of the board of doctors at the Arezzo General Hospital.

The committee's report, published in the Vatican daily *L'Osservatore Romano* of 3 April 1971, gave details of the various scientific tests undertaken and the following results which were established.

1. The blood is real blood and the flesh is real flesh.
2. The flesh is composed of cardiac muscle tissue.
3. The blood and the flesh belong to the same human species.

4. Both blood groups of the flesh and of the blood are the same (hence they came from the same person).
5. The proteins in the blood have been found to be normally fractionated with the same percentage ratio as they are found in the serotherapeutic table of fresh and normal blood.
6. In the blood, there are also chloride, phosphorus, magnesium, potassium and sodium in a reduced amount, while calcium is present in larger quantity.

The report ended with conclusive photographic documentation and later appeared in the highest medical journals in Italy. Professor Linoli stressed that the hypothesis of forgery was entirely without foundation and explained why this was so in considerable detail.

Thus in our de-Christianised twentieth century, a portion of that Heart "burning with love for men"[7] is seen as the seat of that great manifestation of God's love — the Holy Eucharist.

NOTES

1. cf. John Haffert, *The World's Greatest Secret,* p. 205 (A.M.I. Press, Washington, N.J., U.S.A.).
2. cf. *Our Lady of the Most Blessed Sacrament,* by St. Peter Julian Eymard.
3. Père Lamy (1853-1931) was a French priest, called by his bishop "a second Curé of Ars."
4. Recorded in the Italian Blue Army magazine *Il Cuore della Madre,* January 1978.
5. This command was given in a letter by the Pontiff on 12 October 1274, epitomising the voice of the Council of Lyons.
6. cf. *Saint of the Mass,* by Francis Johnston, Catholic Truth Society, London, 1977, and *Alexandrina: the Agony and the Glory* by Francis Johnston, Veritas Publications, Dublin, 1979.
7. Words of Our Lord to St. Margaret Mary Alacoque.

IX

DAILY DUTY

OUR LADY'S pleas for amendment of life, prayer and sacrifice in atonement for our sin-drenched century echo like a constant refrain in her message and we have seen how the three children responded to her requests with an ardour and intensity that was almost unbelievable. They understood the malignity of sin with a supernatural insight, seeing it not only as a trapdoor to the abyss of eternal fire, but as a black response to the pure light of God's love. They never tired of praying and making sacrifices for the conversion of sinners. "I was hungry and didn't eat, but offered it for sinners," Jacinta confided to Lucia when she was very ill. "In the night I had pains and I offered Our Lord the sacrifice of not turning over in bed and because of that, I didn't sleep at all." Francisco would also strive his utmost to console God whom he had seen "so sad" and "in agony until the end of the world," to borrow Pascal's vivid phrase. "Does He still remain so sad?" the little boy would ask Lucia. "I am so sorry He is sad like this. If only I could console Him." Frequently he would spend long hours praying alone in church or in the fields behind walls or bushes, as if keeping watch with his Lord in Gethsemane.

Our obligation to pray and do penance in atonement for others' sins springs from St. Paul's doctrine of mutual responsibility and the common destiny of mankind. (It need hardly be pointed out that reparation made for others' sins must all the more count as reparation for our own sins). Although the passion of Our Lord was more than sufficient to redeem us, that does not prevent that "Christ continues His suffering until the end of the world" through the members of His Mystical Body. "If one man suffers anything, all the members suffer with it." (1 Cor. 12:26). Since we are one with Christ in His Mystical Body, we therefore become saviours of each other, as the doctrine of the Communion of Saints teaches. Hence we must collaborate in the work of redemption and so "complete what is lacking in Christ's sufferings on behalf of His Body, which is the Church." (Col. 1:24).

Explaining this doctrine, Dr. Joachim Alonso, C.M.F., of Madrid, stated on 20 February 1974 in a homily at Fatima: "Inserted as we are in the Mystical Body of Christ, we are, through Him, as one in solidarity with our brethren; first naturally with our saintly brothers in the Communion of Saints, but also with our brothers who are sinners, and with the sin of our brothers. We are one in grace and one in sin." Earlier, Pope Paul VI had expressed the same dogma in his encyclical on Indulgences thus: "A supernatural solidarity reigns among men. A consequence of this is that the sin of one person harms other people, just as one person's holiness helps others." We have already seen dramatic evidence of this in the lives of the three children. The crime of the Administrator of Ourém in imprisoning them resulted in a lessening of the solar miracle which, in turn, reduced the impact of Our Lady's message and in consequence, has imperilled the lives of all of us today. On the other hand, the heroic sanctity of the three children has drawn untold multitudes closer to God. "The little seers of Fatima have won the love of the world," declared Bishop A. Nwedo, C.S.Sp., of Umuahia, Nigeria, "and the life of little Jacinta has tremendous influence on our young people."[1]

This collective responsibility of individuals also applies to nations. Two striking illustrations of this truth were given to us at Fatima. Our Lady urged us to pray and sacrifice ourselves for the conversion of Russia. If we neglected this, we would suffer severely from that country's sins of atheism, as well as from our own sins. Secondly, since Portugal had been given so much grace through the prodigies at Fatima, a greater response to Our Lady's message was expected of that country. "Pray then and do penance," said Cardinal Cento. "Make reparation by voluntary mortification for your own sins and the sins of others. These are the means of resurrection and salvation, the two anchors that will save humanity from shipwreck. Let this message of Mary be put into practice, especially by you, people of Portugal, all the more obliged to do this because of the greater favours you have received from her maternal hands."[2]

Could it then be that a misunderstanding of the above doctrine has been a contributory factor, perhaps even a subconscious one, to the difficulty experienced by some in accepting the full relevance of Our Lady's message? A few years ago, the Blessed Virgin's words "Pray, pray a great deal and make many sacrifices for sinners, for many souls go to Hell because they have no one to pray and make sacrifices for them," were deleted from an article by a theological censor (who happened to be a high ecclesiastic), on the grounds that salvation depended on the individual, that he alone was ultimately responsible for his eternal destiny. The author of the article then drew attention to the words of Pope Pius XII underscoring the above doctrine: "A tremendous mystery this and never sufficiently meditated on — that the salvation of many depends on the prayers and sacrifices made for this intention by the members of the Mystical Body of Christ."[3]

Elsewhere in the same encyclical the pontiff wrote: "If ever we must unite our sufferings to those of our Divine Redeemer for the salvation of souls, so much the more in these days." During the 1960s Cardinal Tisserant, then Dean of the Sacred College, once said: "Each good action helps another person to salvation; each sin compromises the salvation of the world. From the first moment of her meeting with the little shepherds, the Virgin of Fatima spoke directly to them of this serious duty of every Christian."[4]

Despite the incredible penances of the three children, the message of Fatima nowhere specifies such rigorous sacrifices. It is clear that more was expected of the children on account of the unprecedented graces they had received. We can be fairly certain that had we been the recipients of such stupendous manifestations, we would be striving day and night to reform our lives beyond our imagining. *"If men only knew what awaits them in eternity,"* as Jacinta used to say, *"they would do everything in their power to change their lives."* But since we remain unenlightened, at least relative to the children, the penance that God asks of us is simply to persevere in doing His Will and accept all the sufferings and difficulties encountered in the vicissitudes of life.

When Blue Army leader John Haffert asked Sister Lucia in 1946 what Our Lady meant by the word sacrifice, the seer answered: "By sacrifice, Our Lady said that she meant the faithful fulfillment of one's daily duty . . . The rosary is important because we must pray it if we are to fulfil our daily duty . . . The Five First Saturdays' devotion is also important because if people make them, they will purge themselves of sin once a month and renew their purpose to fulfil their daily duty."[5] Lucia later added: "All that God wishes in the way of mortification is the simple, dutiful performance of one's everyday tasks and the acceptance of their difficulty and tedium . . . Many people imagine that penitence means the practice of great austerities and as they have neither the strength nor generosity to undertake such austerities, they are discouraged and fall into a life of indifference and sin. Our Lord has said to me: 'The sacrifice that each one can make is to do his duty and obey my law. That is the form of penance I now demand.' "

Put succinctly, God is asking us to offer up as penance the sacrifices necessary to avoid sin — a far from easy task in our present pagan environment. It means unswerving fidelity to our religious obligations, performing our daily tasks to the best of our ability, being honest, truthful, patient and charitable in our dealings with others and being constantly on guard against temptation, especially as regards the custody of our eyes. Since "a man has only to look upon a woman to lust after her and he has already committed adultery with her in his heart,"[6] and since Our Lady told Jacinta "the sins that lead most souls to Hell are sins of the flesh," the permissive society of today becomes an acute challege to all committed Christians. Pope Pius XII gave us trenchant words of advice that represent a verbal suit of armour. "Our Saviour demands of us above all that we never consent to any sin, even internally, and that we steadfastly remove far from us anything that can even slightly tarnish the beautiful virtue of purity. In this matter, no diligence, no severity can be considered exaggerated."[7]

The importance of daily duty in the cause of world peace may, perhaps, seem rather far-fetched to unbelievers, but it was emphasised by none other than Sir Winston Churchill in one of the most significant speeches of his illustrious career. Addressing 14,000 scientists at the Massachusetts Institute of Technology on the eve of the signing of the N.A.T.O. treaty in 1949, Sir Winston repeated virtually the same words as the message of Fatima. "The supreme question," he declared, "is how we live and grow and bloom and die and how far each life conforms to standards which are not wholly of space or time. Here I speak not only to those who enjoy the blessings and consolations of revealed religion, but to those who face the mysteries of human destiny alone. The flame of Christian ethics is still our highest guide. To guard and cherish it is our first interest, both materially and spiritually. *The fulfillment of spiritual duty in our daily lives is vital to our survival.* Only by bringing it into perfect application can we hope to solve for ourselves the problems of this world — and not of this world alone."

Besides the unspectacular but quietly effective routine of daily duty well done in a spirit of penitence, other opportunities arise, of an equally meritorious nature, for offering sacrifices to God. Pain and sickness are immediately obvious, but there are lesser inconveniences common to everyone such as weariness, humiliation, disappointment, frustration, tension, even weather not to our liking: all these, no matter how small, can be turned to our advantage by offering them to God with the sacrifice-prayer taught by Our Lady on our lips, remembering that it is not so much the size of the gift which counts, but the willingness with which it is given.

This constant striving to sanctify each day in a spirit of penitence will draw down copious graces on the world, making us more effective instruments of God's will in the betterment of mankind, especially in the important sphere of ecumenism. "We should exercise all our activity in union with Christ," explained Cardinal Bea, "humbly submissive to Him, dependent on him and living in Him. Union with Christ however, demands great purity in our actions and in our life, great sanctity and the greatest love and fidelity in taking up our cross each day and following Jesus crucified . . . In fulfilling the message of Fatima, we are collaborating with Mary in the reconstitution and reconstruction of unity between all the baptised."[8]

The same vision was developed even further by Cardinal Baggio, Prefect of the Congregation of Bishops: "In the context of the whole Fatima message, which is an urgent and moving invitation to penance, to the sanctification of suffering, to prayer, to purity, to peace, to the struggle against sin which is a preview of the wonderful conversion to God of man and of peoples who militate against His Church: in this, we glimpse a reflection of the heavenly Jerusalem as it is described by St. John."[9]

NOTES

1. cf. *Seers of Fatima,* 1/1964.
2. Legate of Pope Paul VI: homily in the Cova da Iria, 13 May 1965.
3. cf. *Mystici Corporis Christi.*
4. cf. *Soul* magazine, special edition.
5. cf. *Russia will be converted,* AMI Press, Washington, N.J., U.S.A., 1956.
6. Matt. 5:28.
7. cf. *On Holy Viriginity.*
8. Late head of the Secretariat for Christian Unity. From his homily at Fatima, 13 May 1964.
9. Homily to 700,000 pilgrims at Fatima, 13 May 1976.

X

THE ROSARY

TO HELP us persevere in offering up our daily duties year in and year out, Our Lady urged us to practice the two most powerful and privileged sacramentals in the Church — the rosary and the brown scapular of Our Lady of Mount Carmel. The potency of these two simple devotions in the cause of world peace may be dismissed by some as mere pious sentiment,[1] but in the case of the rosary at least there is solid historical evidence, as we shall see, that the beads are far mightier than the sword.

All Christians are agreed on the priority of prayer in life. It is man's communication link with God. It identifies the soul with the source of infinite power and influence. "Prayer is fundamental to our Christian life," said Cardinal Madeiros of Boston, in a homily at Fatima on 13 May 1977. "Without it, our faith loses its vigour, and hope its dynamic quality . . . Men will not recognise one another as brothers if they have not God for their Father . . . Through prayer, the Christian draws near to God. He becomes fully conscious of his dignity and noble condition as a son of God, and in this way he nurtures a firm confidence in the transcendence, fullness and richness of his faith."

As we have seen, the prayer inculcated repeatedly by Our Lady of Fatima was the devout, daily recitation of the rosary. And with good reason. In the rosary, we have the most powerful and efficacious of all prayers because it is primarily a "gospel prayer" as Pope Paul VI called it in *Marialis Cultus*. The Our Father was given us by Christ Himself and contains "all the duties we owe to God, the acts of all the virtues and petitions for all our spiritual and corporal needs," as St. Louis de Montfort explains.[2] The first part of the Hail Mary was inspired by the Holy Spirit at the Incarnation and at the Visitation, while the latter half was added by the Church at the Council of Ephesus in 430 A.D., when Our Lady's role as Mother of God was defined. The Glory be to the Father is a hymn of praise to the Holy Trinity. And at the end of each decade as we have seen, Our Lady asked us to recite the prayer: O my Jesus, forgive us our sins, save us from the fire of Hell and lead all souls to Heaven, especially those most in need.[3]

Many Catholics, of course, retain their traditional adherence to "the most divine of prayers after the holy Mass and the sacraments," as St. Charles Borromeo called the rosary. Yet it cannot be denied that a sizeable proportion of the faithful now consider the rosary outmoded in this surging, post-Conciliar age. The pleas of Our Lady of Fatima,[4] the insistent appeals of over fifty popes and countless saints and scholars down the ages for its daily recitation, are blandly ignored. The objection frequently heard is that Catholics are becoming more and more oriented to the liturgy, making the rosary obsolete. Another argument claims that the repeated recitation of Hail Marys is monotonous and out of step with the forward march of dynamism and spiritual creativity in this space-age Church. Hence it should go the way of Friday abstinence and the Latin Mass.

These views are not only at odds with factual experience — they contradict the stressed teaching of every modern pope. In his encyclical *Marialis Cultus,* Pope Paul VI devoted almost one third of its length to the relevance and importance of the rosary. And at the height of Vatican II, Pope John XXIII declared that "the sweeping changes appearing in every sector of modern society are arousing a new awareness, even of the functions and forms of Christian prayers. Now every man who prays no longer feels alone . . . but perceives . . . that he is part of a social body, sharing its responsibilities . . . In this way, the rosary assumes the dignity of a great public and universal prayer to express the day to day needs of the Church, of nations and of the whole world."[5] A few years earlier, Pope Pius XII vigorously reminded us that the rosary is the sure remedy given us by Heaven "for the healing of the evils which afflict our times." And Pope John Paul I, while Cardinal Patriarch of Venice, had this to say: "Namaan the Syrian disdained the simple bathing in the Jordan. Some do as Namaan saying: 'I am a great theologian and a mature Christian, steeped in the Bible and in the liturgy through and through, and they talk to me about the rosary.' Yet the fifteen mysteries of the rosary are also the Bible and so are the Our Father, the Hail Mary and the Glory — they are the Bible united to prayer that nourishes the soul. A Bible studied on the mere level of investigation could only nourish pride and empty it of its value. It is not rare for specialists of the Bible to lose their faith."[6]

Even Protestants are coming to recognise the value of the rosary, as instanced by a number of favourable writings, the formation of rosary circles in Anglican churches and the active propagation of the rosary by the Anglican shrine of Our Lady of Walsingham. A German Lutheran minister, Richard Baumann, stated in the early 1970s: "In saying the rosary, truth sinks into the sub-conscious like a slow and heavy downpour. The hammered sentences of the gospel receive an indelible validity for precisely

the little ones, the least, to whom belongs the kingdom of Heaven
. . . The rosary is a long and persevering gaze, a meditation, a
quieting of the spirit in the praise of God, the value of which we
Protestants are learning once more." A Methodist minister, J.
Neville Ward, praises the rosary as a salutary aid to prayer and
meditation in his book *Five for Sorrow, Ten for Joy* and admits that
Protestants have lost much in their neglect of this prayer. Dr.
James A. Beebe, Methodist theologian and president of Allegheny
College in America, agreed with this conviction and admitted to
his students that Protestant prayer suffered because it lacked a
system of controlled meditation. Yet another example concerned
the Protestant minister, Max Broussard, who was so edified by the
rosary and the scapular that he became a Catholic priest and is
now in the diocese of Lafayette, Louisiana.

To suggest then that the rosary is out of date is not only to reject
the pleas of Our Lady of Fatima, but more seriously, to infer that a
prayerful meditation on Christ's life is no longer valid. Nor need
the rosary be a difficult prayer to recite well, as some complain.
Just as ease comes with familiarity, so the daily recitation of the
rosary and meditation on the sacred mysteries of the New Testament will gradually accustom our minds to the scenes and lessons
of each decade. The Annunciation, for example, will evoke the
humility of Our Lord and His Mother; the Visitation, charity; the
Nativity, poverty and detachment from our materialistic environment; the Presentation, obedience to the Church; and the Find-
ing in the Temple, humble acceptance of the trials sent to us by
God. These are just a few of the many lessons we may glean from
meditating on the Joyful Mysteries alone. In practice, "the rosary
comprises all the essential mysteries of Christianity," as Pope Leo
XIII wrote, himself the author of no fewer than twelve encyclicals
on the rosary. "Help me," said Cardinal Koenig of Vienna at the
Rosary Reparatory Crusade at Wiener Stadthalle, Austria on 14
September 1975, "so that the rosary will be recited daily in every
Austrian household and we will have then resolved all our pastoral
problems."

This great prayer not only imparts a deeper awareness and
understanding of the meaning and relevance of Our Lord's life,
but it fans the flame of Divine Love in the soul and through the
Immaculate Heart of Mary, draws us ever closer to the Sacred
Heart of Jesus. Its relevance to the tumultuous problems besetting
the Church and the world today is such that it is fast becoming
known as the "layman's breviary". Cardinal Cento called it "the
prayer of predilection, the Divine Office of the Christian people,"
in a homily at Fatima on 13 May 1965. For its devout, daily recitation brings the gentle Christ to the forefront of our lives, allowing
His healing influence to radiate around us as we put into practice

the virtues learnt from the mysteries. "The rosary is the finest of all prayers," avowed St. Francis de Sales, and his words were splendidly echoed by Pope John Paul II in his Angelus message on 29 October 1978:

"The rosary is my favourite prayer," His Holiness said. "A marvellous prayer! Marvellous in its simplicity and depth. It can be said that the rosary is, in a certain way, a prayer-commentary on the last chapter of the constitution *Lumen Gentium* of Vatican II, a chapter which deals with the wonderful presence of the Mother of God in the mystery of Christ and the Church. Against the background of the words *Ave Maria,* there passes before the eyes of the soul the main episodes of the life of Jesus Christ and they put us in living communion with Jesus through, we could say, His Mother's Heart. At the same time, our heart can enclose in these decades of the rosary all the facets that make up the life of the individual, the family, the nation, the Church and mankind, particularly of those who are dear to us. Thus the simple prayer of the rosary beats the rhythm of human life."

Among the many other authoritative voices appealing for a general return of the rosary, one in particular deserves to be heard with respect — that of Sister Lucia, whom Our Lady of Fatima designated to be her "continuing voice." Her penetrating words deserve the serious reflection of all.

"We must try as much as possible to make reparation to Our Lord through an ever-increasing intimate union with Him so that we identify ourselves with Him and He becomes in us the Light for the whole world which is drowning in the darkness of its error, immorality and pride . . . As a prayer which unites us more intimately with God, the praying of the rosary is second only to the sacred Eucharistic liturgy, because it consists of a wealth of prayers, all of which have come from Heaven, either dictated or inspired by God — the Father, the Son or the Holy Spirit. Moreover, at the end of each mystery, we pray the Gloria which was dictated by God the Father to the angels when He sent them to sing that His Word had just then been born as man: it is a hymn to the Holy Trinity.

"The Our Father was taught us by God the Son; it is a prayer addressed to God the Father. The Hail Mary is entirely impregnated with trinitarian meaning. The first words were dictated by the Father to the angel when He sent him to announce the mystery of His Word's Incarnation: Hail Mary, full of grace, the Lord is with you. You are filled with grace because in you dwells the source of that same grace; it is through your union with the Blessed Trinity that you are full of grace. Moved by the Holy Spirit, St. Elizabeth said: Blessed are you among women and blessed is the fruit of your womb (Jesus). You are blessed because blessed is the fruit of your womb, Jesus. Inspired also by the Holy Spirit, the Church has added: Holy Mary, Mother of God, pray for us sinners, now and at the hour of our death.

"Moreover, the Hail Mary is truly a trinitarian prayer because Mary was the first live temple of the Blessed Trinity. The Holy Spirit shall come upon you and the power of the Most High shall overshadow you. Therefore the holy Child to be born of you shall be called the Son of God.

"Mary is the first living tabernacle where the Father enclosed His Son. Her Immaculate Heart is the first monstrance which held Him. Her lap and arms were the first altar and the first throne on which the Son of God made Man was worshipped. There, the angels, the shepherds and the wise men adored Him . . . Consequently, next to the sacred Eucharistic liturgy, the rosary is the one prayer which introduces us more intimately to the mystery of the Blessed Trinity and of the Blessed Eucharist, as well as the one which brings us closer to the spirit of the mysteries of faith, hope and charity . . .

"The rosary is a prayer for the poor as well as the rich; the learned as well as the ignorant. When souls are deprived of this devotion, then they are deprived of their daily spiritual bread, for this prayer will sustain in a soul that little flickering of faith that has not yet been completely extinguished from many consciences. Even for those souls who pray without meditating, the simple act of taking up the beads to pray is already a remembrance of God and the supernatural.

"The simple remembrance of the mysteries in each decade is another radiance of light which will sustain the smoking torch in their souls. This is why the devil is waging such a great war against the rosary. And what is worse is the fact that he has succeeded in deceiving many persons who occupy positions of great responsibilty. They are blind men leading blind men. They pretend to base their views on the Council and do not realise that the Holy Council ordered them to preserve all the practices that, in the course of years, have been fostered in honour of the Immaculate Virgin Mother of God. The prayer of the rosary, or five decades, is one of the most important prayers and according to the decrees of the Holy Council and the orders of the Holy Father, one we must maintain.

"I hope that the day is not too far off when the prayer of the holy rosary, or of five decades, will be proclaimed a liturgical prayer, because all its parts share the holy liturgy of the Eucharist. Let us pray, work and sacrifice and trust that 'finally, my Immaculate Heart will triumph'."[7]

NOTES

1. In the early part of the thirteenth century, St. Dominic, St. Francis of Assisi and St. Angelus the Carmelite accidentally met one day on a street corner in Rome (a chapel still stands at the spot to commemorate this event). St. Dominic then uttered a famous prophecy: "To my Order, the Blessed Virgin will entrust a devotion to be known as the rosary and to your Order, Angelus, she will entrust a devotion to be known as the scapular. One day, through the rosary and the scapular, she will save the world." The story is found in a book on the scapular by Fr. Marianus Ventimiglia, published in 1773 in Naples.

2. cf. *The Secret of the Rosary*, 12.

3. This prayer has since been authorised by Rome, 4 February 1956, *Office of Indulgences*, 878:567.

4. It is worth remembering that during the first apparition, Our Lady used the word *must* to Francisco, telling him he *must* pray "many rosaries" if he wished to enter Heaven.

5. cf. *Encyclical letter on the Rosary*.

6. Article in the Italian Blue Army magazine *Il Cuore della Madre*, January 1978.

7. Letter to Mother Martins, 16 September 1970.

XI

THE IMMACULATE HEART OF MARY: REPARATION

THE third essential element of the Fatima message — devotion to the Immaculate Heart of Mary — takes two forms: reparation and consecration. On 13 June 1917, Our Lady showed the three children her thorn-wreathed Heart and said: "God wishes to establish in the world devotion to my Immaculate Heart." Note that *God wishes* this devotion. At the same time, the power of the Immaculate Heart shone forth by securing for her children the vision of Hell (which had been denied the world in the parable of Dives and Lazarus) and the miracle of the sun (which had been denied the world in the days of Noah, the last time that mankind was threatened with extinction). She also reassured her children in the most tempestuous hour of history, of her ultimate triumph over the enemies of God and a period of universal peace.

Yet how many have characterised her merciful intervention at Fatima as irrelevant or inconvenient? How many have spurned the shining symbol of her maternal love and care of which Christ Himself was the first beneficiary? How many have removed her statues from our churches, deleted her name from the curriculums of our schools, and from our traditional hymns? How many have cast away her rosary in defiance of Vatican II and the expressed teaching of more than fifty popes? Writing in the periodical *Seers of Fatima* in 1967, Fr. Louis Kondor, S.V.D., refers to the "blindness of many hearts" in this regard and adds: "Indeed, the scribes and doctors of the law abound in this vast Catholic world, who persist in underestimating that fount of graces which is devotion to the Immaculate Heart of Mary, as Fatima has been announcing for over fifty years. Not even the coming of Pope Paul VI, the first of the pilgrims for the golden jubilee, sufficed as a criterion of credibility for such exacting intellects."

As if this were not enough, outside the Church the Mother of God is blasphemed in art, literature, music and the mass media, while her suffering Son is set up as a 'superstar'. On 18 May 1961, the statue of Our Lady of Charity in Havana, which had been proclaimed Patroness of Cuba on 10 May 1916 by Pope Benedict XV, was publicly desecrated amid sacrilegious jeers. Other reported outrages around the world do not lend themselves to words, but an appalling incident in Italy will serve to underline the extent of human malignity towards the Blessed Virgin. Shortly after the attack on Michaelangelo's *Pieta* in May 1972, a dozen of the foremost artists at the Biennal of Venice requested that the Biennal prize be awarded to the attacker of the *Pieta*. Says Fr. Werenfried van Straaten, the famous "bacon priest", in a recent circular: "A relentless persecution is being directed against the Mother of God precisely in an epoch that has most need of her." Pinpointing a significant area of this persecution inside the Church, Dr. Rudolf Graber stated on 23 September 1973 at the Fatima Congress in Freiburg, Germany: "The maturity of the laity is spoken of and even priestly ministry for women; but when it is a question of that Woman who, as a lay person, was elevated above the angels . . . the true cult and veneration due to her is denied under the pretext that such honour should be paid to God alone. At the same time, the human person is exalted to the same transcendental God, identifying Him with Christ. What strange inconsistencies!"

In August 1971, some of the world's leading theologians, led by Cardinal (then Fr.) Ciappi, O.P., papal theologian, resolved at the end of the Blue Army international seminar on the Immaculate Heart of Mary at Fatima that "they have recognised the timeliness and alas, the tragic actuality of the reparation demanded at Fatima . . . for offences committed towards the person of the Immaculate Heart transpierced on Calvary. Doubts cast upon the Immaculate Conception, the perpetual virginity, the divine and spiritual maternity of Mary, as well as a too-frequent rejection of her images and even her displacement from the hearts of children in catechism, constitute an offence of extreme seriousness to God." One of the participants of that seminar, Dr. André Richard, D.D., later commented: "The crisis in the Church comes especially because too many priests, on the pretext of concentrating upon Jesus, have put aside Mary. The eviction of the mother has cast a shadow on the holy humanity of Jesus, upon the truth of the Incarnation of the Word of God, upon the Real Presence in the Host. At the same time, the Church has been devalued as the Mystical Body of Christ, as the spouse without stain or tear already realised in Mary. That is why our times are so sad and menacing. The message of Fatima was given us now to clarify what must be done. The mother has been put aside, humiliated, dishonoured before her children. And there is no home without a mother. There is no family of God without Mary, and that is why Jesus has wished for an extraordinary degree of reparation to be given *now* to Mary."[1]

This reparation is "imperative, obligatory, and in more urgent need than ever," says the renowned theologian Karl Rahner, S.J.

in *Seers of Fatima,* 2/1972. And Our Lady herself spelt out the form that this reparation should take. On 10 December 1925 she appeared to Sister Lucia in her convent at Pontevedra. At her side stood the Child Jesus enthroned on a cloud of light and displaying His Sacred Heart.

After a few moments the Child Jesus spoke to Sister Lucia as follows: "Have pity on the Heart of your most Holy Mother. It is covered with thorns which ungrateful men place therein at every moment and there is no one to remove them by an act of reparation." Our Lady then held out her thorn-wreathed Heart and said: "See, my daughter, my Heart, surrounded by thorns with which ungrateful men wound it at every moment by their blasphemies and ingratitude. Do you, at least, console me and announce that I promise to assist at the hour of death with all the graces necessary for salvation, all those who, on the first Saturday of five consecutive months, confess, receive Holy Communion, recite five decades of the rosary and keep me company for fifteen minutes while meditating on the mysteries of the rosary, with the intention of making reparation to me."

The First Saturday devotion to the Immaculate Heart of Mary antedates this vision, but because of Our Lady's promise of special assistance at the hour of death, the devotion has spread rapidly all over the world. However, before examining this devotion further and answering the several important questions raised by this vision, an overview is necessary regarding the scriptural and historical background of the devotion and its theological basis. This is important since, as there appears to be some misunderstanding regarding the cult, it needs to be demonstrated that it rests, not on the 1925 vision, but on solid theological grounds.

Devotion to the Immaculate Heart of Mary has its roots in the earliest days of the Church when the first Christians pondered Luke 2: 19, 51 and the prophecy of Simeon (Luke 2:35), who foretold that a sword of sorrow would pierce Our Lady's soul. Early Christian writers such as Origen and St. Ephrem, and later, St. Peter Canisius, identified the heart as the seat of intellectual life. A number of the Fathers, followed by theologians and writers, regarded the Heart of Mary as "the core of her sensitive and spiritual life." But, as Cardinal Ciappi, O.P. stated in August 1971 when expounding the doctrine at the above-mentioned international seminar, "the patristic-theological basis for devotion to the Immaculate Heart of Mary has not given us clear testimonies of a specific and distinct cult in ancient times." From the eleventh century onwards however, there is abundant evidence of a growing cult, notably in the writings of St. Anselm, his disciple Eadmero, St. Bernard, Hugo of St. Victor, Richard of St. Lawrence, Ernest of Prague and the great Cistercians Matilde of

Magdeburg, Matilde of Hackborn and St. Gertrude. From there to Fatima there has been a "crescendo of light" says Cardinal Ciappi, "not indeed in the public official Marian revelation — which was closed with the last book of the New Testament — but in private revelation deserving of only human faith, even when rendered legitimate by numerous and spectacular heavenly signs."

St. Gertrude was followed by Rubertine of Casale and St. Bernadine, who merited the title of Doctor of the Immaculate Heart of Mary on account of his commentary on the seven words of Mary. The devotion was further enhanced by St. Francis de Sales and Mary of the Incarnation and climaxed by St. John Eudes who, in 1648, had a Mass and Office composed in honour of the Heart of Mary. It is significant that St. John Eudes's teaching was later closely parelleled by that of Vatican II in *Lumen Gentium*, chapter 8.

He wrote:"Since our salvation has been wrought in this Heart and through this Heart, it is evident that after God and His Son Jesus, this is the first foundation from which we cannot separate ourselves without incurring the evident danger of ruin and of eternal damnation."[2] Though St. John Eudes never formally advocated reparation to the Immaculate Heart of Mary, it is certainly implicit in the wider context of the devotion which he advocated and propagated with such tireless zeal. The cult of consecration however was given special emphasis by the saint: he requested that all churches and chapels of his congregation be consecrated to the Sacred Hearts of Jesus and Mary.

Devotion to the Immaculate Heart of Mary is therefore based on firm historical grounds which have their roots in scripture. As for the theological truths contained in the Fatima revelations concerning this devotion, we can do no better than quote Cardinal Ciappi's words at the above mentioned seminar:

"Sins are an offence, not only against God, but also against the most Sacred Heart of Jesus and the Immaculate Heart of Mary, because sin is principally an offence against God's love and mercy for man, an offence against the sensitive, spiritual and divine love of Jesus, an offence against the maternal and merciful love of Mary for mankind. Now the physical hearts of Jesus and Mary are the symbols of such love and to them are due the cult of reparation.

"Besides penance, both interior and exterior, as a special and very effective form of reparation for such sins, there is also consecration, first of all to the most Sacred Heart of Jesus, Man and God, and then to the Immaculate Heart of Mary, united with Jesus in the work of salvation. The love of Mary for God, as well as for the human race, lies, in fact, at the source of her work as Mother of the Word, and as co-redemptrix with Jesus. To Mary, suffering with her Son, we could well apply by analogy the profound words by which St. Thomas sums up the theology of human salvation when he says, 'one satisfies fully for the offences, when he offers to the injured person something that he (the offender) loves in an equal or deeper way than the hatred he experienced for the pain endured. Thus Christ, in accepting the passion through charity and obedience, offered to God a higher good than it was demanded to compensate for all the offences of the human race. Now the head and the members form one Mystical Body. Therefore the satisfaction of Christ belongs to all his faithful who are members of His body. Moreover, as two persons are united in charity, one can satisfy for the other.' (Summa Theologica, P.III, q 48, a.2,c.). It is, therefore, the charity of Mary suffering with Christ — a charity symbolised by her Immaculate Heart filled with sorrow on Calvary and at Fatima — that lies at the source of her expiatory and co-redemptrix action.

"The Sorrowful Heart of Mary, as it appeared to the three little shepherds in the Cova da Iria, was a symbol of the true compassion, spiritual and sensitive, experienced by the Virgin Mother when 'she stood near the cross of Jesus on Calvary'. It is also the symbol of the most perfect aversion that the Immaculate Heart of Mary, though glorious in Heaven, still feels, even if there be no sensitive or spiritual sadness . . .

"How then can one speak of reparation and of bringing consolation for the offences committed against the Immaculate Heart of Mary? Certainly not in the way our actions of reparation might have been unforeseen by her while suffering with Christ. Unlike her Son, she does not seem, in fact, to have been endowed with any beatific vision on this earth. But we can think that our acts of reparation — recitation of the rosary, acts of mortification both spiritual and corporal, Communions of reparation, consecration — while they place our hearts in accord with the Immaculate Heart of Mary and therefore in a spiritual aversion, ever more sincere and profound, in regard to whatever can offend the most Holy Trinity, the Heart of her Son and her Immaculate Heart, at the same time bring to her physical glorious Heart a true sensitive joy, and an increase of accidental glory to her soul immersed now in the beatifying vision of God . . .

"The Second Vatican Council has not contradicted in any way the theological substance of the message of Fatima, even though the Council has not expressly spoken of the devotion and consecration to the Immaculate Heart of Mary. Rather, one may see a solemn, even though implicit confirmation in the words with which the Constitution Lumen Gentium has exalted Mary for the charity with which she has co-operated in the birth of the children of the Church. Mary is so extolled by the Council as to be recognised in an eminent and absolute way, a most unique member of the Church, the Church's model and most excellent ideal of faith and charity. Even the practice of consecration to the Immaculate Heart of Mary has received praise in the Pastoral Notes with such words: 'The sacrosanct Council deliberately teaches this Catholic doctrine and at the same time exhorts all the children of the Church to generously promote the devotion, especially in liturgical acts, towards the Blessed Virgin, and to hold these practices and exercises of piety in her honour in great esteem, as recommended down through the centuries, by the magisterium of the Church.'

"Finally, the same emphasis has the warm exhortation of the Council in regard to the devotees of Fatima. 'The faithful should remember that the true devotion does not consist either in a certain credulity or in a sterile and passing sentimentalism, but that it proceeds, indeed, from true faith, by which we are brought to recognise the pre-eminence of the Mother of God and are urged to filial love towards our Mother and to the imitation of her virtues.'

"Hence the message of Fatima was turned over to the entire world through the simple and honest little shepherds, by the very one who was filled with the Holy Spirit and who pronounced the Magnificat — a true hymn of love and prophecy, of spiritual triumph for the people of the Messiah. This message is actual still today, and perhaps more so now than in 1917. Today, in fact, even more than in the past, the Catholic Church, the Christian confessions, the nations and the whole world have the need and the duty — even if they do not advert and recognise them — of believing and loving God, of being converted from every form of iniquity, hatred and injustice, and of assuring the triumph of truth, justice, liberty and fraternal charity.

"Against atheism, both theoretical and practical, and especially against that which declared itself militant, it is necessary to oppose the consecration to God of the whole world, and especially to Russia, the principal exponent of such atheism. Now the consecration to the most Sacred Heart of Jesus and the Immaculate Heart of Mary are the easiest and most effective means of living the Christian life. It is through the propagation of such a consecration, sincerely lived, that the prophetic words of the Virgin will be verified: My love will triumph."

Hence "it is urgent for us to establish in the world devotion to the Immaculate Heart of Mary" as Cardinal Larraona, papal legate of Pope John XXIII, said at Fatima on 13 May 1962. *God wishes it,* Our Lady told us. Our efforts must therefore multiply: we must be assiduous in practicing the First Saturdays devotion of reparation, not just once, but continually, for those who do not or will not heed Our Lady's pleas. There is a note of deep spiritual earnestness in Jacinta's words to Lucia concerning this devotion. "I am going to Heaven soon, but you must stay here to make known God's wish to establish in the world devotion to the Immaculate Heart of Mary. Do not be afraid to tell it. Tell everyone that God gives us all graces through the Immaculate Heart of Mary, so that everyone may ask her. Make it known that the Sacred Heart of Jesus wishes that the Immaculate Heart of Mary be honoured with Him. People must ask for peace through the Immaculate Heart of Mary, for God has confided the peace of the world to her."

In a letter dated 12 June 1930, Sister Lucia answered several questions that had been raised concerning the Five First Saturdays reparatory devotion. She revealed that Our Lord had told her that confession within eight days of the First Saturday would suffice, providing that the Communion is made in a state of grace and with the intention of making reparation to the Immaculate Heart of Mary. The Five First Saturdays were in reparation for the five kinds of offences and blasphemies uttered against Our Lady which required reparation. These were: blasphemies against the Immaculate Conception, against her virginity, against her divine maternity and refusal to recognise her as mother of men, blasphemies by those seeking to alienate children from her, and in reparation for those who outrage Our Lady in her sacred images.

We hear of these sins almost daily, as if Satan, knowing his time is short, is waging an all-out war against the Woman destined to crush his head. It is therefore imperative that we practice not only the Five First Saturdays, but the Nine First Fridays devotion in reparation to the Sacred Heart of Jesus. If our faith means anything to us, it means this: that in the present dark hour, when Christ is crucified with an unprecedented malice and intent, we take our stand with the broken-hearted Mother at the foot of the cross and implore pardon and mercy for a sin-drenched world. "So terrible is the sin that weighs upon us," says dramatist Reinhold Scheider, "so terrible the outrage of generations, so terrible the wrath of God, that only a life that is consumed in prayer and penance could avail and cause the light to shine once more in the abyss."[3]

How long then will we continue to relegate the message of Fatima to the restricted category of a private revelation where it can be conveniently ignored? "What Our Lady said to the three shepherds in 1917 holds good for all men at all times," says a collective pastoral letter issued by the Bishops of Portugal on 29 June 1966. How long will it be before the reparatory devotions above are preached and practiced every month in our churches with the priority they deserve? How long will it be before we respond with the alacrity and earnestness demanded by so grave an obligation — for the work of reparation is the pressing responsibility of every committed Christian. Such are the questions we need to ponder seriously while time and life remain.

NOTES

1. cf. *Soul* magazine, May-June 1978.
2. cf. J. Ganderon: *Le Tres Saint Coeur de Marie. Son influence sur le salut et la sanctification des ames d'apres le B. Jean Eudes,* Paris, 1922, p. 75.
3. cf. *Seers of Fatima,* March-April 1974.

XII

THE IMMACULATE HEART OF MARY: CONSECRATION

IN requesting the consecration of Russia to her Immaculate Heart, Our Lady implied that we prepare for this act by our personal consecration to her. To unite ourselves to the Blessed Virgin is to identify ourselves more closely with all her children who are our brothers through her. Above all, it joins us more intimately to Christ, the first born of her children. "The more a soul is consecrated to Mary," says St. Louis de Montfort, "the more it is consecrated to Christ."[1]

We signify our consecration to the Immaculate Heart of Mary by enrolment in and by wearing the brown scapular of Our Lady of Mount Carmel, the 700-year-old sign of personal consecration to the Mother of God. In a famous interview on 15 August 1950, Sister Lucia was questioned by the Very Reverend Howard Rafferty, O.Carm., a provincial director of the Third Order of the Carmelites in America. After stressing the importance and significance of the scapular in the Fatima message, she explained how, during the miracle of the sun when the three children were privileged to see the mysteries of the rosary in tableaux form, the Blessed Virgin appeared as Our Lady of Mount Carmel and held out the brown scapular to the world.

Fr. Rafferty asked Lucia: "Why do you think Our Lady appeared with the scapular in the last vision?" The seer replied: "She meant that all Catholics should wear the scapular as part of the Fatima message. One could not follow this message unless he or she wore the brown scapular." She was then asked: "Is the scapular as important as the rosary in fulfilling the Fatima message?" Her reply summed up seven centuries of devotional history: *"The scapular and the rosary are inseparable."* Following another question, she added: "The Holy Father has told this to the whole world, saying that the scapular is a sign of consecration to the Immaculate Heart of Mary." She was here referring to a letter written by Pope Pius XII in commemoration of the seventh centennial of the scapular in 1951. His Holiness wrote: "Take this scapular which Our Lady has given as a sign of consecration to her Immaculate Heart. Go out and convince the world that it must be dedicated to the Blessed Virgin if it will find peace. Go out and through this scapular re-dedicate families especially to the Holy Mother of God, who has shown her graces so abundantly through this scapular."

For over seven hundred years, millions of Catholics all over the world have regarded the brown scapular with esteem and reverence and worn it in token of Our Lady's celebrated promise to St. Simon Stock on 16 July 1251: "Take this scapular: it shall be a sign of salvation, a protection in danger and a pledge of peace. Whoever dies wearing this garment shall not suffer eternal fire." St. Robert Bellarmine explains the promise as meaning that "whoever dies wearing the emblem of Mary will receive the grace of final repentance." (Obviously, to abuse the promise by sinning at will with the intention of dying in the scapular is a grave evil, for God is not mocked. Our Lady is not promising that those dying in mortal sin will be saved; rather that those dying in the scapular will not die in mortal sin.)

The documentary proof of St. Simon's vision has been sustained by seven centuries of sacred tradition, the teaching of successive popes and saints and countless miracles (recorded in some 300 books). "I learnt to love the scapular Virgin from the arms of my mother," Pope Pius XI admitted.[2] And Pope Leo IX cried out, when his scapular was removed in preparation for his robing as pope: "Leave me Mary, lest Mary leave me!"

"This most extraordinary gift of the scapular is a great incentive . . . to the faithful to follow Mary with a very special devotion," observed Pope Pius IX.[3] And on 2 February 1965, Pope Paul VI wrote to the President of the Mariological Congress held in the Dominican Republic, giving his famous commentary on the Second Vatican Council's *Lumen Gentium,* paragraph 67. (The latter had stressed that the Council "admonishes all the sons of the Church that the cult, especially the liturgical cult of the Blessed Virgin, be generously fostered and that the practices and exercises of devotion towards her, recommended by the teaching authority of the Church in the course of centuries, be highly esteemed."). His Holiness wrote: "Ever hold in great esteem the practices and exercises of devotion to the most Blessed Virgin which have been recommended for centuries by the Magisterium of the Church. And among them we judge well to recall especially the Marian rosary and the religious use of the scapular of Mount Carmel." Hence, to challenge the scapular devotion is, to some extent, to challenge the authority of the Church.

Down through the centuries, the scapular devotion has established a firm and cherished place in the heart of the Church. The Germans revere it as the *grace garment* while the English-speaking world venerates it as *Mary's sacrament.* "Let all of you have a common language and a common armour," urged Pope Benedict XV, "the language the sentences of the gospel, and the common armour the scapular of the Virgin of Carmel which you all ought to wear."[4]

On being validly enrolled in the scapular (any priest now has this faculty), we become clothed in Our Lady's livery and become mystically united to her, thus giving her our homage of service and praise. We place ourselves under the protection of her mantle, so to speak, and show confidence in her ability to help us in these difficult days by her powerful intercession. "It is not enough to say that the habit of the Blessed Virgin is a mark of predestination," said Blessed Claude de la Colombière. "It is more than a sign of true devotion to Mary. Because of the alliance which Mary contracts with us and which we contract with her, no other devotion renders our salvation so certain."[5]

In wearing the scapular, we should strive to imitate Our Lady's beautiful spirit of recollection, humility, purity, patience and charity, so that God may see the likeness of His own Mother shining in the souls of His children. "Like St. John of the Cross," says Fr. Rafferty, "all of us who make the commitment of belonging to Our Lady in a special way by taking the scapular and wearing it faithfully must be resolved also to imitate all the virtues of which this holy habit is a symbol." In this way, our consecration to the Immaculate Heart of Mary becomes an *internal* act as well, resulting in contrition, a firm purpose of amendment and a rededication to the precepts of the gospel. As St. Alphonsus expressed it: "Just as men take pride in having others wear their livery, so the most Holy Mary is pleased when her servants wear her scapular as a mark that they have dedicated themselves to her service and are members of the family of the Mother of God."[6] (The scapular of St. Alphonsus and that of St. John Bosco were found perfectly preserved in their tombs, when everything else had turned to dust, and the scapular of Blessed Gregory X was found perfectly intact in the tomb when the pontiff's remains were exhumed in 1830 — *over 500 years* after his death.)

Those wearing the scapular become eligible for what is known as the *sabbatine privilege*. This is understood to mean that those wearing the scapular, reciting daily the Little Office of Our Lady (or the rosary, in the case of Blue Army members), and observing chastity according to their state in life, will be released from Purgatory on the first Saturday after death (or whatever is the equivalent of the first Saturday in the next life). The privilege is believed to have been based on a bull said to have been issued by Pope John XXII on 3 March 1322 after receiving the favour in a vision of Our Lady. Though the authenticity of the only copy of this bull in existence is not absolutely certain, several subsequent popes appeared to endorse it. Pope Paul V stated: "It is permitted to preach . . . that the Blessed Virgin will aid the souls of the brothers and sisters of the confraternity of the Blessed Virgin of Mount Carmel after their death by her continual intercession, by her suffrages and merits, and by her special protection, especially on the day of Saturday which is the day especially dedicated by the Church to the same Blessed Virgin Mary."[7] From this it seems that the Church is willing to accept that such souls will be released from Purgatory soon after death, and especially on a Saturday. Pope Benedict XV endorsed this belief when speaking about the scapular to the seminarians of Rome. "It enjoys," said His Holiness, "the singular privilege of protection even after death."[8] In 1916, he granted an indulgence of 500 days each time the scapular was devoutly kissed. And Pope Pius XI said in a letter of 18 March 1922, commemorating the sixth centenary of the sabbatine bull: "It surely ought to be sufficient merely to exhort all the members of the confraternity to persevere in the holy exercises which have been prescribed for the gaining of the indulgences to which they are entitled, and particularly for the gaining of that indulgence which is the principal and the greatest of them all, namely that called the sabbatine."

NOTES

1. *True Devotion to Mary*, 2:1.
2. cf. Letter written to mark the 6th centenary of the Sabbatine privilege, 18 March 1922.
3. cf. Preface written by Pope Pius IX to *La Vie de St. Simon Stock* by A. Monbrun.
4. *Sign of her Heart* by John Haffert, p. 74.
5. From Sermon pour la Fête, *Oeuvres*, (Lyons, 1702), t. III.
6. *Glories of Mary*, t. 2, p. 374.
7. cf. Analecta O. Carm, vol. 4, p. 250.
8. Discourse given on 16 July 1916.

XIII

THE PILGRIM VIRGIN

ONE OF the most effective means of spreading the message of Fatima has undoubtedly been the world-wide circulation of Pilgrim Virgin statues. These images of Our Lady of Fatima are deployed at national, diocesan and parish level in many countries while an International Pilgrim Virgin statue travels all over the world. A statue, of course, is like a sculpture; it is not an idol, but merely a symbol of what it represents. No honour is due to it, nor given to it. When we salute the Cenotaph in London we are not honouring a pillar of stone, but the memory of the Fallen in the wars, which the pillar symbolises. "The Pilgrim Virgin conveys the moral presence of Our Lady," says Fr. Joseph Cassidy, D.D., Ph.D., of the archdiocese of Newark, U.S.A. "Moral presence is not the same as physical presence, but rather implies the *effect* of her real presence." This effect has been so striking that the Pilgrim Virgin programme has become part and parcel of the Fatima story itself. "Experience shows that a visit of the statue of Our Lady of Fatima in the diocese results in a true shower of graces," observes Professor A. Martins, S.J. "Any priest who doubts this need only volunteer to sit in the confessional during one of the visits of Our Lady's statues. You cannot do better than to promote the diocesan and parish visits of Pilgrim Virgin statues as a way to draw all to the devotion of the rosary and the First Saturdays."[1]

The Pilgrim Virgin saga began in 1942 when the statue of Our Lady of Fatima in the Cova da Iria was taken to Lisbon for a Catholic Youth Congress. Such was the upsurge of faith and conversions that a second journey was made to the city in 1946. On this occasion, white doves let loose by someone in the crowd fluttered down to rest at the feet of the statue and remained there for days without food or drink, oblivious to the jostling crowds, blaring bands and the long road and river journey back to Fatima. The "miracle of the doves" as everyone called it, was later repeated in Brazil during an imposing ceremony in honour of Our Lady of Fatima.

On 13 May 1946, Pope Pius XII sent Cardinal Masella as his legate to Fatima to solemnly crown the statue as "Queen of Peace." The crown, which weighed 1,200 grammes, was a gift from the women of Portugal who contributed their jewels totalling 950 diamonds, 313 pearls, 17 rubies, 14 emeralds, 269 turquoises and 2,650 precious stones, in thanksgiving for Portugal's preservation from the Spanish Civil War and the Second World War. The following year a new image known as the International Pilgrim Virgin statue of Our Lady of Fatima was blessed in the Cova da Iria and sent on a world-wide visitation which persists to this day.

Right from the start, the journey of this statue was accompanied by such spectacular signs that Pope Pius XII exclaimed: "As she sets forth to claim her dominions, the miracles she performs along the way are such that we can scarcely believe our eyes at what we are seeing." The statue was brought to America that same year by Canon de Oliveira of the diocese of Leiria-Fatima and John Haffert amid indescribable scenes of joy and emotion. As the procession bearing the statue left the Cova da Iria for New York, crowds of pilgrims "pressed in from all sides, trying to kiss the statue, many with tears streaming down their cheeks," Mr. Haffert recalled.[2] When the plane reached the Azores, a crowd which had waited up all night to see the statue burst into the plane to pay their respects to Our Lady. A few hours later, the airport at New York witnessed its biggest-ever passenger traffic jam as thousands surged forward for a glimpse of the "white lady of peace". All across North America, immense multitudes thronged to greet the statue; more than one third of the entire population of the city of Buffalo turned out to welcome Our Lady of Fatima. In Ottawa, 100,000 people filled the university stadium and 200 priests joined in a solemn ceremony of crowning and consecration. Midnight Mass was celebrated simultaneously in 124 churches in the archdiocese. "Within one year," wrote John Haffert, "the Pilgrim Virgin has evoked the greatest Marian public demonstration this nation has ever seen. Four million people had touched the image . . . making four million acts of faith in the conversion of Russia."

Similar scenes were repeated throughout the world as a second Pilgrim Virgin statue travelled through the other four continents accompanied by miraculous cures and political miracles. The welcome in Spain was, perhaps, even more stupendous than in America. Recalling this memorable triumph in the *Voice of Fatima,* August 1951, Bishop Vicente of Solsona wrote: "In all small parishes and working class colonies, an average of 95-97 per cent received the Sacraments. The average for the whole diocese was 90 per cent . . . The visit of Our Lady of Fatima to our diocese has been, in truth, a mission . . . and has borne fruits of sanctification more abundantly than the best organised mission heretofore. It has been a diocesan mission, the results of which would be difficult to exceed . . . A missionary son of the Immacu-

late Heart of Mary told us after the beginning of the pilgrimage:
'We do not need any more missionaries. The Blessed Virgin by her
presence alone achieves more than all of us with our preaching
and labours.' This supernatural fruit, the achievement of the
pilgrimage, claimed the attention of all and provoked intense dis-
cussion. Priests in particular were surprised and astonished. We
saw many of them overcome with emotion to the point of tears.''

When the statue reached the Spanish-French border, it opened
for the first time in more than a decade and has remained opened
ever since. All across Africa and Asia, millions flocked to venerate
the statue and learn of Our Lady's 'Peace Plan from Heaven'.
Moslems, Buddhists, Hindus and Sikhs were particularly enthusiastic. The Moslems, who have a certain devotion to Our Lady
and recognise her Virgin birth and Immaculate Conception, were
intrigued by the fact that Mary had appeared at Fatima, which was
the name of Mohammed's favourite daughter and regarded by the
prophet as the highest woman in Heaven after Our Lady. In Zanzi-
bar, the Moslem sultan placed a wreath of flowers at the statue's
feet, while the Moslem chief of the Ismaeli tribe in Mozambique
placed a golden necklace about the statue's neck saying: "Thank
you, Our Lady of Fatima for the work of love you are accom-
plishing in Africa. We praise you, together with the Almighty
Allah." When the Pilgrim Virgin reached Kenya, the chief of the
ferocious Mau Mau insurrection was converted. Crossing the Gulf
of Arabia the Pilgrim Virgin arrived in India and on that very day,
the murderous civil war between Hindus and Moslems ceased and
peace negotiations were opened. Buddhists greeted the statue with
almost the same enthusiasm as Catholics, recognising Our Lady as
the mother of him whom Buddha had prophesied in his *Diamond
Sutra.*

"Five hundred years after my death will appear One who will
fulfil all righteousness. One who has the root in him not only of
one, two , three, five, ten, or one thousand Buddhas, but of ten
thousand Buddhas. Therefore when he comes, hear him." Four
hundred and forty-five years later, Our Lord was born in
Bethlehem. Elsewhere in the sub-continent and other parts of
Asia, vast multitudes of non-Christians venerated the Pilgrim
Virgin with the same astonishing enthusiasm. As one old Hindu
was heard to say: "She has shown us that your religion is sincere; it
is not like ours. Your religion is a religion of love; ours is one of
fear."

In 1954 Pope Pius XII issued his encyclical *Ad Coeli Reginam,* in
which he saluted the Pilgrim Virgin statue as "the messenger of
Mary's royalty", and stated that in the doctrine of Our Lady's
Queenship lies the world's greatest hope for peace. These words
need to be recalled and pondered on by many today. Our Lady

herself had said in 1917 that "only she" could obtain peace for the world from her Divine Son, the Prince of Peace.

When Pope John XXIII decided not to divulge the famous third secret of Fatima in 1960, there was an understandable, yet unjustified reaction and falling off in devotion to the message of Fatima, but the impetus of former years is now fast recovering. In 1967, a number of new Pilgrim Virgin statues were blessed by Pope Paul VI and delivered by the Blue Army to the national hierarchies of twenty-one countries. Immense crowds once again greeted Our Lady of Fatima, especially in Tokyo, Taiwan, Saigon, Bangkok and the Philippines. Four years later, the Blue Army took seventy further statues to individual nations. In war-torn Vietnam, some three million turned out in Saigon to welcome the statue. Just outside the city the vehicle carrying the image was unaccountably halted and, acting on an inspiration, the people built a shrine at the spot, dedicated to Our Lady of Fatima. Recently, reports from refugees, confirmed by the priest-secretary of the apostolic-delegate in Saigon, indicate that the shrine has been the scene of apparitions and wonders. Our Lady is said to have made a number of prophecies; the most talked-of is that "by 1980, the crowds coming here will be very great."

When Cardinal Luciani (the future Pope John Paul I) asked Sister Lucia in 1977 whether she thought Our Lady would be pleased if a Pilgrim Virgin statue was carried through Italy, the seer replied with a vigorous affirmative. Shortly after, the statue was flown from Fatima to the Vatican and just before Pope John Paul I died, it began a two-year journey through the country at the tomb of Padre Pio. The tour may yet prove to be the much-loved Pope's greatest legacy to his sorely-tried country.

In April 1978, the Blue Army took the International Pilgrim Virgin statue round the world in a special plane called "Queen of the World" on the most ambitious venture yet to help spread the Fatima message, fulfilling a century-old prophecy by St. Catherine Labouré: "One day, Our Lady will be carried around the world in triumph." Many millions greeted the famous image all across the Far East, climaxed by an all-night vigil of prayer at the frontier of South and North Korea attended by 30,000 people. At Taipei, capital of Taiwan, over 800 bishops, priests, nuns and monks followed by an immense concourse of people took the statue on a motorised float into the city. The government of Singapore gave the statue a diplomatic reception and Archbishop Gregory Yong led countless thousands in prayer before the image.

After a trail of tumultuous triumph in Thailand and India, the statue finally arrived in Cairo and permission was requested of President Sadat of Egypt and Prime Minister Begin of Israel to fly it direct to Jerusalem. President Carter and many American senators and congressmen were urged to support this request, for there was no civil air-link between Cairo and Jerusalem. While permission was awaited, the statue was enshrined at the Church of Our Lady of Fatima, Heliopolis, the traditional spot where the Holy Family took refuge from Herod. Nearby was the celebrated Coptic-Orthodox Church of St. Mary, Zeitoun, where millions from all over the world had reportedly seen Our Lady as a living figure of light over a two and a half year period.[3] In the presence of the statue, concelebrated Mass was offered by the Patriarch of Cairo, Cardinal Sidarouss, assisted by many other prelates and leading Protestant churchmen. Shortly afterwards came word from President Sadat: "Permission is granted for the Queen of the World plane to fly tomorrow direct from Cairo to Jerusalem." Prime Minister Begin had already given the plane permission to land in Israel and the first civil airline flight between the two capitals was extensively covered by American TV networks.

On arrival in Jerusalem, the Patriarch of the city issued a pastoral letter, *The Holy Land, Our Lady's Land,* and invited all Christians to join in greeting the symbol of Our Lady of Fatima at the Church of the Holy Saviour, near Calvary. In his homily, the Patriarch welcomed the statue to "the city of Mary" where she had undergone so many eventful experiences during her life on earth. Next day the statue flew into Rome to a stupendous welcome from over one million people. Thousands walked through the entire night, praying all the time, to the shrine of Our Lady of Divine Love where the statue was first taken, and the morning Mass by Cardinal Poletti, Vicar of Rome, was attended by hundreds of thousands of Romans. Pope Paul VI sent the following message through his Secretary of State, Cardinal Villot: "The Holy Father expresses deep happiness over the solemn Marian ceremonies . . . He hopes that Romans will continue to show their centuries old and ardent devotion to Our Lady through Christian living, always consistent with the gospel message." The statue was then taken to the Basilica of St. John Lateran where it was greeted by a crowd of almost unprecedented size, even for the Eternal City. "So great was its gesture of love, as witnessed by incalculable thousands of pilgrims," wrote Ronald Singleton in the *Universe* of 19 May 1978. "The three and a half foot white statue seemed to take on a life of its own . . . The old and young came to witness. Students mixed with military men. Tourists from every country in Europe came to pray. For two and a half days this year, Rome's ration of terrifying violence gave way to peace . . . The statue's last visit in June 1959 attracted hundreds of thousands. Now on this occasion, the promises and revelations made to three little Portuguese shepherds seemed even more urgently apt . . . The Holy Father's words for the occasion were a simple and sweet sermon, throwing grave political days into startling relief: 'A disciplined Marian cult expressing spontaneous delicious sentiment and reflex of heart . . . an ideal model of perfection . . . the model of a sublime mother, gentle, saintly, a mirror of goodness. Mary, as every Christian knows, is the intercession all can obtain . . . is the 'pray for us' which should never be missing from our lips.' "

Vatican Radio continued to broadcast the message of Fatima and the story of the Blue Army to the world as the statue left for Vienna and Budapest. On arrival at Warsaw Airport, the communist authorities forbad the statue to leave the plane. "Do not hold this against Poland," Cardinal Wyszynski told the Blue Army leaders. "You have left Our Lady of Fatima a prisoner at the airport, but I am sure she is not unaccustomed to restrictions." The Polish Government were subsequently so embarrassed that all nineteen of the other countries which had been visited around the world had accepted the statue, that they asked the Blue Army to return with the Pilgrim Virgin in 1979. Cardinal Wyszynski countered by asking permission to construct the first churches in Warsaw since the war. Finally the government agreed and on 10 January 1979, John Haffert presented Pope John Paul II with a cheque to help pay for the first church, appropriately named Our Lady Queen of the World.

After a brief visit to Berlin, the statue was flown to Lourdes where there was a repetition of the "miracle of the doves." Thousands jostled around the image for two days without disturbing the doves at Our Lady's feet: they only flew off as the statue was being taken to Tarbes Airport for its flight to Fatima to be present at the ceremonies in the Cova da Iria on 13 May. The round-the-world pilgrimage had ended and countless millions had greeted the famous statue and learnt of Our Lady's message, or heard the Fatima story from the many broadcasts in seven languages by Vatican Radio.

The importance of the Pilgrim Virgin apostolate on national, diocesan and parochial levels is difficult to underestimate. As we saw earlier, many of the visitations seem to have an almost miraculous effect in rejuvenating the Faith in the area. The report of Father E. Brodeur of St. Stanislaus Kostka parish in the Marquette Diocese, America, is typical. "It is now four months since Our Lady's visit. I am giving more instructions than I've ever given in my thirteen years as a priest, more confessions, more returns to the Church, more going to Mass and Communion regularly, more Christian charity."[4]

"The greatest fruit of the Pilgrim Virgin has been conversions . . . numbered in many, many thousands," wrote John Haffert in his best-selling book *Russia will be Converted.* "I met a Belgian

priest in Fatima on 12 October 1947, who had come from Belgium
in a pilgrimage of thanksgiving because of the number of conversions in his parish . . . where the statue had been for twenty-
four hours. He told me that in Charleroi, one of the most com-
munist-infested cities of Belgium, 62 priests were hearing confessions, even on the sidewalks, and that there were 55,000 Communions. One of the priests, with tears in his eyes, said: 'I never
expected to live to see so much grace at one time touch men's
hearts.' "

That Our Lady of Fatima seems to speak to us again through her
moral presence signified by the statues is underlined by numerous
reports from various countries of such statues having been seen to
shed tears and even tears of blood. While the Church has never
undertaken a formal investigation of any such reported prodigy, in
at least one case, chemical analysis of the weeping fluid has confirmed that the tears are genuine. Typical of such reports was the
front page headlines of *Le Matin,* largest secular newspaper in
Haiti, on 28 May 1976:

*Phenomenon in a church. Tears running from the eyes of a statue of
Our Lady.*

The report stated: "A considerable crowd filed into the chapel
of Our Lady of Fatima following rumours that tears had flowed
from the eyes of a statue of the Blessed Virgin. Very excited, the
curious crowds wanted to see for themselves whether it was true or
false . . . Those able to get close to the statue have indeed stated
that there was a drop of water under the right eye. Was it a tear, as
most of the witnesses proclaimed — or simply a drop of humidity
caused by the heat? But, of course, statues don't perspire . . . Witnesses stated: 'She cries because of our sins. There are too many
vices in the city.' "

Eighteen months later, on 1 January 1978, the International
Pilgrim Virgin was seen to weep in Las Vegas. The mayor of the
city, William H. Braire, wrote: "One could sense something was
happening as everything in the Cathedral was quiet. There was no
movement of any kind except a man pointing to the statue . . . a
priest moving to closely view the face . . . I myself looked very
closely and very carefully to convince myself that what I saw was
true: *moisture coming from the eyes of the statue.* Moisture had
gathered in the lower part of the eye. The only further proof I
could have sought was by physically touching the moisture on the
eye and cheek. This I did not do out of a reverend respect for the
person represented by the statue."[5]

Though final pronouncement on the authenticity or otherwise of
such phenomena rests with the Church, at least one archbishop in
America has stated that a reported weeping statue in New Orleans

"could be genuine." In 1977, the Bishop of Damascus sent the Blue Army in America four sworn documents testifying to the weeping of the National Pilgrim Virgin statue of Syria, which continues to this day (November 1979). Wrote Mgr. Dr. Georges Hafouri, pastor of the Church of Our Lady of Fatima, Damascus:

"A trembling ran through my whole being when I saw tears flowing from the eyes of the statue. They did not roll down in big or small drops as our tears might do, but seemed rather to be like a dense perspiration coming directly from the eyes of the Virgin, particularly the left eye, which was visibly dimmed with tears and contracted. His Excellency, the Most Rev. Angelo Pedroni, Pro-Nuncio Apostolic, arrived, accompanied by his secretary and ecclesiastical chiefs of the Catholic communities of Damascus. The Pro-Nuncio said: 'It is not natural. There is certainly something here.' Television, radio, papers and magazines of Lebanon, Egypt, Jordan and other Arab countries, and even of Europe and the U.S.A., spread the news everywhere — even to Tahiti in Oceania. Many reports and articles have been published in diverse languages. To me, it is particularly touching to see Catholics, Orthodox, Protestants, even Moslems, from Kuwait, Iraq, Jordan, Turkey, and elsewhere, pray with faith and emotion which rival sometimes the faith of our Christians. Fatima is a venerated name with the Moslems. It is the name of the daughter of their prophet Mohammed. That is why they feel a particular sympathy for Our Lady of Fatima. Inspired by their Koran, they have always manifested a true devotion to the Blessed Virgin. *Sitna Miriam*, as they call her . . ."

The other depositions came from the Vicar General of Damascus and two distinguished Catholic doctors in the city.[6] cf. *Soul* magazine, Sept.-Oct. 1979. If so, what else can the tears mean but that Our Lady is expressing, in the most poignant manner possible, the grief she voiced at Fatima over the storm of sins today and the fearful punishment they may unleash from an outraged Divine Justice. Is not rejection of the Fatima message a fulfillment of the words of the prophet: "I called and you did not answer; I spoke to you and you did not listen"? (Is. 65:4).

And who will say that such chastisement may not come when, in the light of Our Lady's warning in 1917 of "the annihilation of various nations," if "men do not stop offending God," we find ourselves confronted by a world of unprecedented wickedness and possessed of terrifying means of mass destruction? Padre Pio, the famous stigmatist priest, had this to say shortly before his death in 1968: "I can give you only one piece of advice for today: pray, and get others to pray, for the world is at the threshold of its perdition."

The message of Our Lady of Fatima is, we repeat once again, a clarion call for the ten just men of this permissive age to stand up and save the city of the world. "It is no longer time to sleep, but to watch in order that humanity be saved," said Padre Pio. "Help yourselves as much as you can with the arms of faith, with the arms of penance, with the arms of shame. Act now to implore pardon and mercy for all the brutalities of the world. Let Marian groups of pious souls, in a spirit of reparation, organise pilgrimages to the sanctuaries of the Madonna, praying the rosary together for God's mercy and pity. The most Blessed Virgin, compassionate Mother, who sheds tears of blood over today's world, calls all her children to penance and prayer. Let these pilgrimages be in a spirit of penance . . . Pilgrimage 'leisure trips' are worthless . . . The time is now the hour of darkness. Therefore increase Marian pilgrimages to counteract the works of Satan and to prepare for the triumph of the Immaculate Heart of Mary. In some parishes, recreational trips are organised. Why not think to organise sacred pilgrimages in a spirit of penance? Let us fear the chastisements of God. Let us give up some licit pleasures. Let us be like a family which, seeing one of its members dying thinks only of prayers to save it. I speak to you thus, not to make you fear, but so that each one may regulate his own conduct to make the world better. If you do not listen, yours is the responsibility."

NOTES

1. cf. *Soul* magazine, January-February 1978.
2. cf. *Russia will be Converted,* by John Haffert, A.M.I. Press, Washington, N.J., U.S.A.
3. From April 1968 to early 1971, Our Lady is believed to have appeared publicly at the Church of St. Mary before immense multitudes of some 250,000 nightly, the majority being Moslems. The visions were officially confirmed by the Coptic-Orthodox Patriarchate, the Head of the Evangelical Church in Egypt (speaking on behalf of all Protestant Churches), the Greek Catholic Church and the Egyptian Government. Cardinal Stephanos acknowledged that it was "a real appearance", and two of Pope Paul's personal investigators saw the vision for themselves. The author is in possession of many books, newspapers and photographs of this extraordinary event which was foretold by a reported vision of Our Lady in Lithuania in 1962.
4. cf. *Soul* magazine, May-June 1979.
5. Ibid.
6. cf. *Soul* magazine, Sept.-Oct. 1979.

XIV

TIME FOR ACTION

HOLDING up his rosary before an immense multitude in the Cova da Iria on 13 May 1966, Cardinal Ferreto forcefully urged compliance with the message of Fatima and added: "She wants all of us to work on the apostolate of evangelisation and sanctification among our brothers, so that the temporal order may be restored in Christ and according to Christ. This is exactly what the Council asked us to do: *That men no longer offend God by sin, but live in grace and sanctity.*"

Over the years, a number of international apostolates have sprung up, dedicated to living and spreading our Lady's message. By far the largest is the Blue Army of Our Lady of Fatima with many millions of members and International Headquarters in Fatima. Its President is the Bishop of Fatima himself.

In 1946, an American priest, Fr. Harold Colgan, lay dying of a heart ailment. In the extremity of his pain, he made a vow to the Blessed Virgin that if she would cure him, he would devote the rest of his life to propagating the message of Fatima. Days later, he walked out of the hospital in perfect physical condition and began his immense task by urging his parishioners at St. Mary's, Plainfield, New Jersey, to respond to Our Lady's requests.

Shortly afterwards, Lucia helped Fr. Colgan's right-hand man John Haffert, who had been an indefatigable scapular apostle in America, to draw up Our Lady's message into a compact pledge which people could sign. The wording was as follows:

Dear Queen and Mother, who promised to convert Russia and bring peace to all mankind, in reparation to your Immaculate Heart for my sins and the sins of the whole world, I solemnly promise: 1). To offer up every day the sacrifices demanded by my daily duty; 2). To say part of the Rosary (five decades) daily while meditating on the mysteries; 3). To wear the Scapular of Mount Carmel as a profession of this promise and as an act of consecration to you. I shall renew this promise often, especially in moments of temptation.

Millions around the world signed the pledge. These were then microfilmed and buried within a few feet of the spot where Our Lady had appeared.

As a daily means of implementing this pledge, Blue Army members are urged to recite the Morning Offering as a positive response to the plea of Our Lady on 13 May 1917:

O my God, in union with the Immaculate Heart of Mary, (here the Brown Scapular is kissed as a sign of one's consecration), I offer Thee the most Precious Blood of Jesus from all the altars throughout the world, joining with it the offering of my every thought, word and action of this day.

O my Jesus, I desire to gain every indulgence and merit I can and I offer them, together with myself, to Mary Immaculate, that she may best apply them to the interests of Thy most Sacred Heart. Precious Blood of Jesus, save us! Immaculate Heart of Mary pray for us! Most Sacred Heart of Jesus, have mercy on us!

To date, many millions around the world have joined this army of prayer and sacrifice. Besides fulfilling the initial pledge, Blue Army members are urged to wear something blue as a reminder of the promise they have given to Our Lady. This recalls the passage in the Old Testament (Numbers 15: 37-41) in which the Jews were urged to wear a blue ribbon to recall the commandments of God.

On 8 May 1950, Fr. Colgan was received in private audience by Pope Pius XII. His Holiness told him: "As world leader against Communism, I gladly give my blessing to you . . . and to all members of the Blue Army." Since then the movement has grown with astonishing rapidity, embracing many high-ranking churchmen including the celebrated Garrigou La Grange, O.P., one of the greatest living theologians in the 1950s.

On 13 October 1956, the International Headquarters of the Blue Army was officially opened at Fatima by Cardinal Tisserant, Dean of the Sacred College of Cardinals and Legate of Pope Pius XII. "Today more than ever," His Eminence declared on that occasion, "Christ wills that we have everything from Him through His Mother, according to the words of St. Bernard recalled recently by the Sovereign Pontiff . . . The Blue Army is a response to the demands of the Blessed Virgin at Fatima . . . Is it not necessary that all Catholics who still enjoy liberty should arrange themselves like an army around Our Lady, stronger against evil than an army arranged in battle, yet tender like the most tender of mothers, if they wish mercy to be poured forth abundantly on sinners? Therefore with all my strength I appeal for a more and more widespread and more popular imploration of Our Lady, certain that only the intervention of the most Blessed Virgin Mary will obtain the necessary graces of conversion and reawaken an authentic sense of unity in Christ and in the Church for a true world peace."

It would take volumes to describe the work of the Blue Army across the world since that landmark. Bishops have been particularly enthusiastic with the apostolate. On 8 December 1960, while the communists were threatening to plunge Guatemala into civil war, Bishop Constantine Luna issued a pastoral letter appealing for compliance with the Fatima Message and the formation of Blue Army centres. Shortly after, when the Congo was torn apart by a murderous, red-instigated civil war, the Archbishop of Elizabethville pleaded with Blue Army members on 7 January 1962 to re-double their spiritual efforts to obtain peace in that strife-torn country. Elsewhere around the world, bishops responded with alacrity to the Blue Army's offer to donate National Pilgrim Virgin statues to any country requesting them. The reaction of the Church behind the Iron Curtain was epitomised by Bishop Tomasek of Prague when he exclaimed to the Blue Army party that delivered the Czechoslovak statue on 17 October 1967: "You have brought us the sign of our hope." (A month earlier, Cardinal Beran, exiled Archbishop of Prague had gone to Fatima to pray for his country).

Today, the work of the Blue Army includes the propagation of Pilgrim Virgin statues, the production of TV films on Fatima (in America), all-night vigils of reparation and the Cell movement. An estimated 10,000 Blue Army members in America alone make monthly all-night vigils. Britain has its monthly vigil on the first Saturday at Tyburn Convent, London, at the spot where the martyrs died in the sixteenth century. The Cell movement, on the other hand, helps to spread the Blue Army's "wave of holiness" in depth at parish level. Two or three members meet once a week to discuss the spiritual state of the world in the light of the Fatima message and to encourage each other to prayer and sacrifice after the example of the three children of Fatima. They practice the prayers taught by the angel and Our Lady and try to become victims for sinners like Lucia, Francisco and Jacinta. When the Cell grows, it divides and multiplies, thus spreading a wave of holiness through the parish.

The Blue Army also runs a flourishing Cadet division for the young (though this has yet to be realised in Britain). Led in America by Fr. Robert Fox, a priest-journalist of the calibre of Don Bosco, the movement has spread to thousands of Catholic children and teenagers across the country. A single issue of *Soul* magazine (May-June 1979) gives a graphic insight into the marvellous work being done by the Blue Army among youth. "I will enter the Carmelite Order in February," wrote a Cadet from Wisconsin who made the 1978 pilgrimage to Fatima. "My brother who went the previous year is now considering the priesthood." A high school student in California wrote: "About 1.00 a.m. each night, a couple of seminarians and I go to Chapel to pray the Rosary. After that, we pray the Angel's Prayer in front of the Blessed Sacrament with our foreheads to the floor, as we did on the pilgrimage to Fatima." "I've organised young people in my neighbourhood into a Cell," wrote another correspondent. "We follow the guidelines of the Cadet Prayer Cell programme, meet each week and use the tools outlined in the Cadet Kit. Our parents serve as adult leaders." Fr. Fox adds: "About 95% of the young people on our Fatima pilgrimages experience a deep spiritual transformation . . . Almost 60 of our young men are now preparing for the priesthood and many young ladies are entering the convent."

Pilgrim Virgin statues . . . all-night vigils . . . the Cell movement . . . the Cadet division: thus does the Blue Army comply with the trenchant words of Pope Pius XII on 4 June 1951: "Do not forget the heavenly Message which you have had the good fortune to hear. Keep it in your heart and translate it into good works which are the surest pledge of the greatest blessings." "Russia will be converted", Padre Pio told John Haffert in the 1960s, "when there is a Blue Army member for every communist".

Today we hear much about the necessity of feeding the hungry peoples of the Third World, but compliance with the Fatima message is even more important because Our Lady promised that the fulfillment of her requests would put an end to world hunger. (Her apparition a century earlier at La Salette, France, stressed that famine, besides war, was also a punishment from God for sin). And on a practical level, the conversion of Russia would liberate immense sums of money currently spent on armaments, to transform the living standards of underdeveloped countries.

The potency of Our Lady's message has been demonstrated on a number of occasions in recent years. When Austria was half occupied by the Russians after 1945, some ten per cent of the population signed a pledge to comply with the Fatima requests. And on the weekend of 13 May 1955, the thirty-eighth anniversary of the first apparition at Fatima, the Russians suddenly agreed to withdraw from the occupied half of the country — *the only time that the communists have ever given up an enslaved population without a shot fired in anger*. One of the Austrian cabinet ministers at the time reportedly exclaimed: "Our liberation is inexplicable, except for the direct intervention of the Virgin of Fatima."

Eleven years later, the communists were so sure of seizing power in Brazil that the party secretary announced to the Moscow International Press the precise day (a few weeks hence) when the hammer and sickle would fly over that vast strategic country. "All key positions were in the hands of notorious communists or pro-communists," recalled Fr. Valerio Alberton, S.J., Vice-Director of the National Federation of Marian Congregations of Brazil. "The penetration went deep into even Catholic faculties. Communist cells were discovered even in our colleges. Neither did Catholic Associations escape. It was terrible." At the eleventh hour a nation-wide rosary crusade was launched; millions implored the Immaculate Heart of Mary to save them. An immense gathering of 600,000 women marched through the centre of São Paulo praying the rosary for three hours. "Mother of God," they cried, "preserve us from the fate and suffering of the martyred women of Cuba, Poland, Hungary and other enslaved nations." Similar scenes were witnessed in other cities. The communist President Goulart, seeing the vast groundswell against him, fled the country. And the red shadow over Brazil lifted.

The experience was repeated in Portugal in 1975. When everyone in the West from Dr. Kissinger down felt that only a miracle could save that country from Communism, the Portuguese people went down on their knees and prayed the rosary as never before, entreating Our Lady of Fatima to save them. The prayer-storm reached its quivering climax on 13 October 1975. Weeks later, the long expected communist coup was almost bloodlessly and decisively crushed. As the Cardinal Patriarch of Lisbon proclaimed at the 8th Fatima Congress at Kevelaer, Germany, on 18 September 1977:

"I can say that it was the consecration made in Fatima to the Immaculate Heart of Mary by the Portuguese bishops in 1931 and 1938 that defended Portugal from the common peril, then so close to its borders. It was the same consecration, renewed in 1940, that saved Portugal from the horrors of the Second World War . . . And certainly it was the great devotion of the Portuguese people to the Virgin Mary, ratified anew by the consecration effected by the bishops on 13 May 1975, which halted the advance of Communism among us, when it had already seized control of many departments of our government and threatened to submerge the whole of the public and private life of the Portuguese people."

This consecration was renewed on 17 June 1979 by the Cardinal Patriarch of Lisbon and the bishops of Portugal on the occasion of the inauguration of a national shrine to the Immaculate Heart of Mary in the crypt of St. Mary's Basilica, Sameiro, near Braga.

A final example occurred in Chile. The communist government of Dr. Allende in the early 1970s was overthrown by a three-year rosary and scapular campaign, and one of the first acts of the new government was to rebuild the national shrine of Our Lady of Mount Carmel. And though a great deal of severe repression still exists in the country, two things must be borne in mind. The communist alternative would have meant a vastly greater repression and secondly, Church leaders in Chile are certainly aware of the need for a deeper spiritual commitment to rectify the curtailment of human rights in the country. "Catholics in Chile urgently need a true application of the Fatima message", said Mgr. Massa Fierro, rector of the major seminary in Valparaiso. Pope John Paul II voiced the same theme at Pueblo, Mexico in February 1979 when he stressed the priority of the spiritual direction to life in the resolution of the daunting problems besetting Latin America.

As we approach the end of this book, we can do no better than epitomise its theme with the words of the great intellectual and Blue Army leader of France, Abbé André Richard, D.D.:

"There are two signs on the horizon of the Church in the twentieth century: Our Lady of the Rosary of Fatima on the charismatic level, and Vatican II on the institutional level. The place which Our Lady held in the Council was outlined on 11 October 1963 at the beginning of the second session. Pope Paul VI had summoned all the Council Fathers to St. Mary Major's in Rome, where he prayed that Our Lady would cause the Church to recognise her as its Mother, its incomparable model, its glory, joy and hope. Then, after promulgating the most important document of the Council *(The Constitution on the Church)* on 21 November 1964, the Pope referred explicitly to Our Lady of Fatima, proclaimed Mary as Mother of the Church, and declared that the doctrine of the Church about Mary is the key for the knowledge of the mystery of Jesus and also of the mystery of the Church. The message of Fatima is so timely with regard to the Council that perhaps it will not show its greatness and fruits until some time in the future . . . In a word, Fatima is clearly up to date in its appeal for conversion. But its timeliness appears even more important as this message from Heaven to the modern world gives a reply to the anxiety increasing more and more in today's world . . . As simple children could believe in the miracle because they saw it, the most advanced minds can begin to believe it because it makes heavenly sense."[1]

To sum up the message and meaning of Fatima: Sister Lucia has stressed, as we have seen, that when a "sufficient number" comply with Our Lady's requests, God would permit the Collegial Consecration. When John Haffert asked her in 1946 whether the conversion of Russia would definitely follow, the seer replied deliberately: "Yes. That is what Our Lady promised". Mr. Haffert responded: "But *when,* Sister, when will it happen?" Lucia replied: "It *will* happen. There might be much more suffering, more nations may be afflicted, but it will happen *when a sufficient number are fulfilling the requests".*

Commenting on this critical need, Bishop Graber had this to say: "Knowing that the world can be utterly destroyed by the terrible weapons of mass destruction today, and knowing too that this can be averted by prayer and penance as the Most Holy Virgin reminded us at Fatima, it is my most sacred obligation to utilise these twin means of salvation: prayer and penance. Neglecting them, I incur guilt in the destruction of the peoples. The omission of prayer and penance — I say this in all seriousness — is a crime against humanity".[2]

In the early 1940s, Sister Lucia reportedly told a Russian girl in exile, Natacha Derfelden (who had gone to the International Youth Congress at Fatima), that the conversion of Russia will be achieved through the Orthodox Church and the Oriental Rite. If this report is correct, and there is evidence that it is, it would seem to heighten the significance of the celebrated Icon of Kazan which we spoke of earlier. This venerated painting played an enormous role in the religious and national life of Czarist Russia and was acclaimed the "Protectress and Liberatrix of Holy Russia". After the 1917 revolution, the Icon was smuggled out of Russia and after being purchased from an art dealer for a huge sum by the Blue Army, it was enshrined for a time in the Byzantine chapel at the Blue Army International Headquarters, Fatima. Now back in America, it awaits the glorious day of its triumphant return to a converted Russia.

The power of the Fatima message was underscored for the whole world during the atomic bomb explosion at Hiroshima on 6 August 1945. A German Jesuit and seven of his colleagues were living only eight blocks from the blinding centre of the nuclear flash, yet all escaped while flaming death screamed around them. To this day, all eight occupants of that building are alive and well while others living some distance away continue to die from the radiation effects of that frightful holocaust. Over the years some two hundred scientists have examined these eight survivors, trying to discover what could have spared them from incineration or the lethal storm of radiation. Speaking on TV in the United States, the German Jesuit, Fr. Hubert Shiffner, gave the startling answer. "In that house the rosary was prayed every day. In that house, we were living the message of Fatima". His words seemed to underline Sister Lucia's statement in 1977: "Our Lady will protect all her dear ones".

Hence, in the very light of the nuclear flash that threatens us all, we can see the sign of our salvation writ large. The Woman "more brilliant than the sun" has intervened in the most critical hour of human history and promised to save the world, stamping her words with "the most obvious and colossal miracle of history". At the same time she dramatically confirmed the faith of the Church in anticipation of one of its greatest spiritual crises in 2,000 years. Surely we will respond to her pleading message and not spurn the hand held out to save us?

We will end with the question that has haunted us all through this book: *when* will the number of people complying with Our Lady's message be sufficient? *When* will the ten just men of this permissive age stand up and by their prayers and sacrifices, save the city of the world? "It will be late", Our Lord told Sister Lucia in 1931, "Russia will have already spread her errors throughout the world, provoking wars and persecutions against the Church. The Holy Father will have much to suffer".

How late depends entirely on us . . . It could be no later than today. Each one of us has the power in our rosary-clasped hands to transform the face of the world, despite the unrelenting cataract of evil surging through our midst. "One just soul can obtain pardon for a thousand sinners", St. Margaret Mary used to say. *That* is the Divine equation of mercy that could have saved Sodom and Gomorrah — and it holds true today.

So let us respond — now.

NOTES

1. cf. *Soul* magazine, January-February 1979.
2. cf. *Seers of Fatima*, 2/1972.

BIBLIOGRAPHY

The literature on Fatima is enormous, and it is only possible to cite here the more important works in English, apart from Sister Lucia's Memoirs, published as *Fatima in Lucia's Own Words* by the Postulation Centre, Fatima, in 1976 (and available in the U.K. from Augustine Publishing Co.).

ALONSO, Rev. M. *The Secret of Fatima; Fact and Legend,* Cambridge, USA, 1979.

BAKER, G. *The Finger of God is here,* St. Paul's Publications, 1961.

BERGIN, R. *This Apocalyptic Age,* Fatima International, 1970.

DA CRUZ, Rev. J. *More about Fatima,* Westminster, USA, 1953.

DE MARCHI, Rev. J. *The Crusade of Fatima,* New York, 1948.

GALAMBA DE OLIVEIRA, Canon J. *Jacinta, the Flower of Fatima,* New York, 1946.

HAFFERT, J. M., *Russia will be Converted,* Washington, USA, 1956.
Meet the Witnesses, Washington, USA, 1961.
Sign of Her Heart, Washington, USA, 1971.
The World's Greatest Secret, Washington, USA, 1964.

JOHNSTON, F. *Have You Forgotten Fatima?* C.T.S., London, 1977.

MARTINDALE, Rev. C. *The Message of Fatima,* London, 1950.

McGLYNN, Rev. T. *Vision of Fatima,* New York, 1951.

McGRATH, Rev. W. *Fatima or World Suicide,* Scarboro, USA, 1950.

PELLETIER, Rev. J. *The Sun Danced at Fatima,* Worcester, USA, 1951.
Fatima: Hope of the World, Worcester, USA, 1954.

RYAN, Rev. F. *Our Lady of Fatima,* London, 1943.

WALSH, W. T. *Our Lady of Fatima,* New York, 1947.

GENERAL INDEX

SUBJECT INDEX

NOTES